Editor
Mara Ellen Guckian

Editorial Project Manager
Ina Massler Levin, M.A.

Editor in Chief
Sharon Coan, M.S. Ed.

Illustrator
Victoria Ponikvar Frazier

Cover Artist
Cheri Macoubrie Wilson

Art Coordinator
Denice Adorno

Creative Director
Elayne Roberts

Imaging
Ralph Olmedo, Jr.

Product Manager
Phil Garcia

Publishers
Rachelle Cracchiolo, M.S. Ed.
Mary Dupuy Smith, M.S. Ed.

Learning Through Movement

Monthly Activities

Authors

Barbara Forslund Cracchiolo, O.T.R.
and Patricia Marie Anderson, O.T.R.

Teacher Created Materials, Inc.
6421 Industry Way
Westminster, CA 92683
www.teachercreated.com

ISBN-1-57690-647-7

©2000 Teacher Created Materials, Inc.
Made in U.S.A.

Table of Contents

Introduction

Children need to *move* to enable themselves to learn. Movement is fun, and it is necessary to encourage growth and development. Children process information from their five senses to help them know where their bodies are in space and how to move to get around in their environment. In early development, our nervous system develops primarily through tactile and motor experiences. (If we sat perfectly still, we would soon fall asleep.) The more immature the nervous system, the more movement and tactile experiences are needed to help it develop.

Success comes with motivation and mastery of a skill. A child needs to feel comfortable with a certain level of mastery of a gross motor skill before we can expect them to have good fine motor control. A child who can draw large circles with whole arm movement on the blackboard or a child who is able to maneuver him or herself around, under, over, or through an obstacle course has a better success rate when it comes to sitting at his or her desk and doing coloring and writing activities. Teaching different concepts using movement helps develop the nervous system in an enjoyable, stimulating manner. It makes learning fun!

This book contains weekly sensory motor activities that can be done in the classroom. Each weekly activity has a theme. These sensory motor activities are geared to preschool, kindergarten, and special education classes. All of the activities in this book have been tried successfully in a number of settings including preschool, kindergarten, and first grade. The classes have included regular education students and special education students. Teachers, physical education specialists, and occupational therapists will find these activities helpful in promoting growth in their students. Gross motor skills, body awareness, spatial relationships, fine motor skills, and motor planning skills are emphasized.

Each weekly theme is explored with a multi-sensory approach. Each is presented with the following:

- gross motor activities that will encourage body awareness, motor planning, and spatial awareness.
- fine motor activities that will encourage tactile experiences, finger and hand control, manipulation of materials, and visual perception.
- sensory motor activities that can be done in the classroom or sent home to parents.

Remember, if you as a teacher are having fun, your students will have fun. Learning to move and moving to learn are fun and challenging to us all.

How to Use This Book

The activities presented in *Learning Through Movement: Monthly Activities* are arranged according to a traditional school year, beginning with September and ending with June. Seasonal activities and holidays are interspersed with topics known to be child pleasers. Each month, or unit, is divided into the following five sections:

Materials—These bulleted lists include all the items needed to present the unit's activities. Optional materials are mentioned when appropriate. It is up to you to determine how much of each item you will need for how many children. Most items can be found at home or are already in the classroom. The remaining materials listed are available at school or art supply stores, or the directions for creating them can be found in the unit. When gathering materials, make note of those needed for each individual and those to be shared by a group.

Teacher Preparation—This section details the things to be done prior to the student's arrival. The directions detail what should be done to set up all the activities on the same day. Room arrangement suggestions are also found in this section.

Directions to Students—The directions in this section read a bit like a script. They are simply worded instructions for teachers to use with their students to ensure their understanding. Use these directions as a starting point to present the activity. Individualize them to meet specific group needs and abilities. Let your imagination and style of teaching guide your presentation.

Keep in mind that directions for each activity are given for the whole class to participate in at the same time. Each activity will take approximately 30 minutes for the whole class to do. (This does not include preparation time.)

If you feel smaller groups are possible, try these modifications:

- Set up small groups of four or five students for each activity or try groups of 10 students at a time with aides or parent volunteers.
- Divide the class in half. Take half the class and start on the gross motor activities while a parent or volunteer takes the other half of the class and starts on the fine motor activities. Then switch activities.
- Choose one activity to do each day from each theme.

Additional Activities—Here, you will find extensions to the activities to continue improving the student skills individually, and as a group. You may also find ideas to enhance classroom learning centers.

Observations for Sensory Motor Activities—This section is the *why* of the book. It gives you, the teacher, specific behaviors to look for to determine whether your students are grasping the skills your activities are targeted to meet. The observations are broken down into five categories—Motor Planning, Body Awareness, Bilateral Integration and Crossing Midline, Tactile Awareness, and Fine Motor—to further help isolate strong and weak areas.

After telling you what to look for, this section explains why it is important. It gives possible explanations for why a student is having difficulty and what adjustments might be made. For example, if a student is not able to sit on a T-stool which you are using to help develop the trunk muscles needed for good sitting posture, it is possible that the stool is too tall. By adjusting the height for that student, you might enable him or her to sit comfortably. Often, just knowing what to look for will help guide your presentation, allowing your students to get the most from their activities.

How to Use This Book *(cont.)*

Motor Planning

Motor planning refers to a student's ability to figure out how to do a new motor task. Some of our motor actions are routine, such as bringing a spoon up to the mouth for eating. If we are asked to bring the spoon to a knee or up to an ear, we would have to think about the movement and plan the motor action. That is motor planning. Prior to any movement the brain has to organize all the environmental information so that the body will move in the direction needed with the appropriate speed, force, and timing. The ability to motor plan depends on thinking skills as well as sensory motor development.

Below are some suggestions for helping students who are having difficulty with motor planning:

- Guide students through the motor action.
- Give one direction at a time.
- Use visual cues.
- Minimize oral and auditory distractions in the room.
- Keep verbal directions to a minimum.
- Have students orally repeat directions.
- Have a check-off sheet for students to check off each step as they complete the task.
- Break tasks down into smaller steps.
- Do a lot of rolling, jumping, and ball activities.
- Play "imitation" games such as Simon Says or Follow the Leader.
- Play games with movement and rhythm.

Body Awareness

Body awareness refers to the student's ability to know where his or her body is in space. Opening jar lids without looking at your hands, gauging how far to duck your head when getting under a low table, and sitting down without constantly looking at the chair all require you to have a good sense of where your body is in space.

Other indicators of a student's sense of body awareness include how close or far away he or she sits from other students and how hard or how gently items are pulled apart or put together. Students who have poor body awareness appear clumsy, walk by shuffling their feet on the floor, have difficulty climbing on playground equipment, and continually bump into other students.

Heavy lifting, pushing, pulling, and carrying all help your brain to know where your body is in space. Other suggestions for helping students who are having difficulty with body awareness are listed below:

- Guide students through the activity.
- Carry a heavy stack of books.
- Take out the garbage.
- Push feet and/or hands against the walls as if to push the walls out.
- Do push-ups and pulls-ups.
- Play tug of war.
- Play on a jungle gym. Start on low equipment and then advance to taller equipment.
- Do frog jumps.
- Play Simon Says.
- Use teetertotters.
- Do jumping activities.
- Swing by lying on the stomach rather than sitting on the swing seat.
- Try beanbag activities.
- Play on the monkey bars.

How to Use This Book (cont.)

Bilateral Integration and Crossing Midline

Bilateral integration refers to the student's ability to use both sides of his or her body in an activity. Sometimes our hands are doing the same movement, and at other times they are acting separately. When catching a ball, both hands are doing the same motion. When coloring or writing, one hand is doing the movement while the other hand is holding the paper.

Crossing the midline refers to the student's ability to cross over the midline of the body. The midline is an imaginary line that runs through the body cutting it in half from head to toe. Crossing the midline is the student's ability to reach with the right hand or right leg over the midline to the left side of the body. Crossing the midline means moving an arm and a leg, not moving the body, and twisting toward one side.

Activities that necessitate using both hands, both feet, or crossing over midline help develop the neuron pathways within the brain for reading, writing, and academics. Coordinating both sides of the body is needed for the development of many gross and fine motor skills.

Below are some suggestions for helping students who are having difficulty with bilateral integration and/or crossing the midline:

- Jump rope.
- Do jumping jacks.
- Practice jumping with feet apart, jumping and landing with feet crossed, and jumping and landing with feet apart.
- Scissor-walk on a line.
- Sharpen pencils using a manual pencil sharpener.
- Turn a hand eggbeater.
- Tie shoes or tie yarn bows on packages.
- Practice cutting.
- Play two-square or four-square.
- Play musical instruments.
- Ride a bike.
- Carry heavy objects with two hands.
- Play clapping games and use rhythm sticks.
- Skip.
- String beads.
- Tear paper.
- Do mixing bowl activities and practice stirring, pouring, and measuring.
- Roll clay.
- Use pop beads or interlocking blocks.
- Wind wind-up toys.
- Play basketball.
- Swim.
- Practice opening snack and lunch containers.

Tactile Awareness

Tactile awareness refers to the student's sense of touch. Skin is the largest sensory area on our bodies. The palms of our hands and the bottoms of our feet are the most sensitive. We are constantly using our sense of touch for everything we do. Tactile receptors are located under the skin all over our bodies. Receptors in our hands help us to know whether an object is soft, hard, hot, cold, bumpy, smooth, etc. Tactile receptors also let us know when a breeze blows across our arms or legs. Tactile receptors in our mouths let us know if there is food in our mouths.

Students who are tactile defensive, or overly sensitive to touch, will be reluctant to touch many materials such as play dough, glue, finger paint, or other messy items. These students may also be very selective of what foods and textures they eat.

How to Use This Book *(cont.)*

Tactile Awareness *(cont.)*

Below are some suggestions for helping students who are having difficulty with tactile awareness:

- Use a firm touch on student's arms, legs, and back rather than a light touch.
- Let student rub various textures on his or her arms and legs.
- Avoid unexpected touching of the student.
- Avoid approaching student from the back; always let him or her see you approaching.
- Let student initiate touch.
- Encourage student to pull and push heavy objects.
- Allow a tactile defensive student to go first or last in line so other students don't rub against them.
- Offer a variety of manipulatives.
- Encourage hand washing.
- Encourage gradual exposure to messy experiences, even if only momentary.
- Provide an escape, like a quiet corner from too much sensation.
- Provide a variety of sensory experiences such as a bean table, water table, or sand table.
- Don't force, but encourage, participation in tactile activities.
- Let student have his or her own personal space when sitting on the floor, such as a carpet square.

Fine Motor

Fine motor refers to the student's ability to use his or her hands to operate tools accurately. Tools commonly used in school include pencils, crayons, scissors, and other manipulatives. Precision is not a matter of strength; it is a matter of coordination of the muscles in the hands. Large arm and hand movements develop before fine precise motor skills develop. We don't expect a three- or four-year-old to hold a pencil correctly and write his or her name. The muscles have not accurately developed yet. If pencil skills are pushed too early, students develop poor habits that are difficult to change when they really need to write which is usually in the first grade.

Below are some suggestions for helping students who are having difficulty with their fine motor skills:

- Emphasize easel and chalkboard activities.
- Shake dice.
- Roll out play dough.
- Use pegs and pegboards.
- Do lacing and stringing activities.
- Use short pieces of chalk and crayons rather than full-sized ones.
- Do finger plays.

- Play with shadow puppets.
- Wash hands.
- Apply hand lotion to hands.
- Eat with a spoon or fork rather than fingers.
- Pick up money and put it in a piggy bank.
- Put small objects in ice cube trays or egg cartons.
- Use tongs to pick up items.

Hand Map

Definitions

finger pads—fingertips (See illustration.)

finger opposition—thumb touches tip of any finger

pincer grasp—looks the same as thumb touching index finger except there is a small object between thumb and index finger.

tripod grasp—pencil is held between pads of thumb and index finger and rests on side of long finger close to the tip

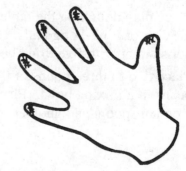

Apples

Materials

- 1 or 2 apples
- apple peeler (old-fashioned apple peeler, corer, and slicer, or regular apple peeler)
- 3" x 24" (8 cm x 61 cm) fabric streamer, one per student
- red, yellow, and pale green construction paper
- clothesline, 6–7 feet (190 cm)
- dried beans, 2–3 pounds (.9–1.3 kg)
- 10 wooden clothespins
- 5 craft sticks
- scissors
- glue
- play dough
- 2 mixing bowls
- measuring cups
- wooden spoon
- 2 chairs

Teacher Preparation

1. Cut out at least 10 apples using red, yellow, and pale green construction paper. Laminate the apples, if possible.

2. Cut the craft sticks in half. Lightly sand the cut edges. Glue one-half of a craft stick perpendicular to the end of each wooden clothespin to make a winged clothespin. (See illustration.) Students use the winged clothespins by placing a thumb on one side and their four fingers on the half craft stick.

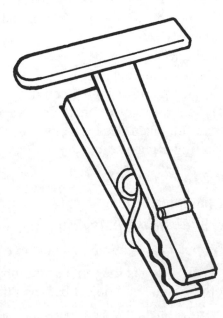

3. Attach a clothesline between two chairs so it is about three to four feet (91 cm–122 cm) off the ground. Place 10 apple cutouts on the clothesline using the winged clothespins.

4. Place one streamer per child on the floor.

5. Place play dough on the table in small balls, about the size of Ping-Pong balls. There should be one per student with five dried beans next to each ball.

6. Place two to three pounds (.9–1.3 kg) of dried beans in a mixing bowl. Place measuring cups, a wooden spoon, and another mixing bowl next to it.

8

Apples (cont.)

Directions to Students

Apple Peel

1. Today we are going to pretend we are apples.

2. Has anyone seen parents or grandparents peel an apple and cut it up to make applesauce or an apple pie?

3. This is an apple peeler (hold the apple peeler up in the air), and this is how you peel an apple. You start at the top and slide the peeler over the skin, digging in slightly at the beginning to get it started. (Try to peel the apple in one continuous strip.)

4. We are going to pretend we are apples being peeled. Watch me. (Hold fabric streamer in one hand above your head. Slowly spin around and slowly bring streamer down the length of your body until it touches the floor.) Now pick up your streamer and pretend you are an apple being peeled.

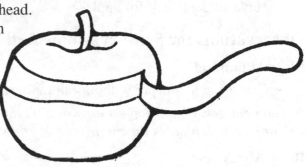

5. Let's try that again. This time hold the streamer in your other hand and turn in the opposite direction. Remember to keep your free hand by your side.

Hanging Apples

1. Come over to our clothesline of hanging apples. How many do we have today?

2. Can you take down one apple? Now try to take down three apples. Can you hold an apple in one hand and a clothespin in the other? Don't let the apples fall to the ground.

3. After you have taken three apples off the clothesline, try to reattach them on the clothesline.

Apple Seeds

1. Let's walk over to the table. Each of you has a small ball of play dough and five beans. We are going to pretend these (dried beans) are apple seeds, and we are going to plant them.

2. Using your pointer finger (hold up an index finger), push the beans in one at a time and cover them up with play dough. After you have planted the seeds, you need to squeeze the play dough and find the five seeds. Take them out. Roll your play dough back into a ball and line up the five seeds for the next person.

Applesauce

1. Now we are going to pretend we are making applesauce. You will need to fill up measuring cups with our ingredients (dried beans) and pour them into another mixing bowl.

2. After you have poured in the apples, water, sugar, and cinnamon (four pours), you need to stir the ingredients with a wooden spoon. Let's practice our stirring motion together. Now, take turns at the pouring station. Are you blending all the ingredients together?

3. Who would like a taste of a real apple after all that work? Take a slice of apple, bite it, and chew it with your back teeth.

Apples (cont.)

Additional Activities

1. Have the students hold onto the streamer with one hand with the other hand on their stomachs. Have an adult spin the student around while holding onto the other end of the streamer to wrap them up. After the student is wrapped up, unwrap them.
2. Have students hang apples, using winged clothespins on real branches.
3. Make applesauce.
4. Read a book about apples. Try *How Do Apples Grow* by Betsy Maestro, HarperCollins Children's Books, 1992.
5. Have streamers in apple colors—red, yellow, and pale green.
6. Have students bob for apples.

Observations for Sensory Motor Activities

Motor Planning

- Can the student spin without falling down?

If a student gets dizzy, suggest crawling on the floor or doing push-ups. This heavy work pattern is calming and eliminates the dizziness.

Body Awareness

- Can the student hold onto a streamer, spin, and bring the streamer down slowly and smoothly to the floor or is it a jerky movement?

If difficult, have the student sit down and move the streamer.

Bilateral Integration

- Can the student hold onto the apples with one hand and the clothespins with the other, or can he or she only hold the clothespin letting the apples fall to the ground?

Have the student work on two-handed activities.

- Can the student put the apple back on the clothesline using the clothespin, or is he or she only able to put the clothespin on the apple and not on both the apple and the clothesline?

If difficult, work more on two-handed activities such as stringing beads or using an egg beater.

Tactile

- Can the student poke dried beans into play dough, or is there reluctance to touch the play dough?
- Can the student pick up and hold a slice of apple, or are hands withdrawn?

If the student withdraws his or her hands, encourage but don't force the student to try to touch the apple.

Fine Motor

- Can the student pour by moving only his or her hand and wrist, or does he or she need to use shoulder and arm movements?
- Can the student pour smoothly and accurately or are beans all over the table? Can the student pour from a large measuring cup to a smaller cup with no spillage?

If difficult, encourage chalkboard activities and other vertical activities.

10

Wheels on the Bus

Materials

- 7" (18 cm) diameter plastic hoop or hula hoop per student
- 1 empty paper towel or toilet paper roll per student
- 1 empty film container with lid per student
- 2 streamers per child or per group
- 1 rubber band per student
- scissors and craft knife
- 3 pennies per student
- 2–3 beach towels
- paper hole-punch
- wax paper

Teacher Preparation

1. To make a cardboard kazoo, use a paper hole-punch to punch one hole 1" (2.54 cm) down from the end of the roll. Place a piece of wax paper on the same end and secure it with a rubber band about ³/₄" (2 cm) from the end.

2. Using a craft knife, carefully cut a 1" (2.54 cm) slit in each film container lid. Place the lid back on the empty film container. Students will put pennies in the containers.

3. Place two or three beach towels lengthwise on the floor. This will be the road on which the students will roll.

4. Place one plastic hoop on the floor per child or per group. Inside each hoop place two fabric streamers, one kazoo, one film container, and three pennies.

The Wheels on the Bus

The wheels on the bus go round and round,
round and round, round and round.
The wheels on the bus go round and round,
all through the town.

The wipers on the bus go swish, swish, swish,
swish, swish, swish, swish, swish, swish,
The wipers on the bus go swish, swish, swish,
all through the town.

The horn on the bus goes beep, beep, beep,
beep, beep, beep, beep, beep, beep.
The horn on the bus goes beep, beep, beep,
all through the town.

The lights on the bus go blink, blink, blink,
blink, blink, blink, blink, blink, blink,
The lights on the bus go blink, blink, blink,
All through the town.

The children on the bus go bounce, bounce, bounce,
bounce, bounce, bounce, bounce, bounce, bounce,
The children on the bus go bounce, bounce, bounce,
all through the town.

Wheels on the Bus (cont.)

Directions to Students

Wheels on the Bus

1. Today we are going to sing the song, "The Wheels on the Bus."

2. First you are going to pretend you are the bus rolling down the road. Lie down on this end of the road (beach towels laid lengthwise) and roll to the other end of the road. Then stand in front of a hoop filled with items to use on our ride.

3. Next, pick up the plastic hoop. As we sing our song, we are going to use the hoop as a steering wheel. Hold the hoop in front of you (demonstrate holding the hoop at 10 o'clock and 3 o'clock, bringing the right hand to 10 o'clock and turning the hoop to 3 o'clock; repeat), and turn it as we sing "The wheels on the bus go round and round."

4. Put the hoops down and pick up the streamers, placing one in each hand. Hold your arms up in the air and wave both arms together back and forth like windshield wipers as we sing, "the wipers on the bus go swish, swish, swish."

5. Put the streamers down and pick up your kazoo. As we sing, "the horn on the bus goes beep, beep, beep," sing the beep into the kazoo.

6. Put the kazoos down and hold your arms up in front of you at shoulder level. When we sing, "the lights on the bus go blink, blink, blink," touch your thumb to your index and middle fingers.

7. When we sing, "the children on the bus go bounce, bounce, bounce," jump in place with your two feet together.

8. Now, let's sing the whole song and do all the body actions.

Paying for the Bus

Note: This next direction is given when the students finish the song.

1. On most buses you pay when you get on the bus, but on our bus we pay when we get off. Pick up the three pennies and put them into the film container one at a time.

2. Shake the filled container as you hand it to the "bus driver."

Additional Activities

1. Have children roll down the road to the right and then have them come rolling back to the left.

2. Have the students keep their arms above their heads when rolling.

3. Pick up the three pennies one at a time, using thumb and index finger. Move the penny to under the middle, ring, and little finger. Have the student do the reverse to place the pennies in film containers.

4. If students can't hold their ring and little fingers down into the palm of their hand when "blinking lights," put a sponge or eraser under those fingers to keep them down in the palm of the hand.

5. Have students make up new verses to the song.

6. Read *The Wheels on the Bus* by Raffi, Crown Publishers, 1998, or by Paul O. Zelinsky, Dutton Books, 1990.

12

Wheels on the Bus *(cont.)*

Observations for Sensory Motor Activities

Motor Planning

- Can the student organize body movements quickly, or is there hesitation?
- Can the student do the motor actions without looking at the other students for visual cues?

If difficult, help guide the student through the motor action. Emphasize jumping, ball activities, Simon Says, and Follow the Leader.

Body Awareness

- Can the student roll in a straight line by staying on the towel, or does he or she roll off to one side?
- Can the student do the blinking motion without looking at his or her hands?
- Can the student do the blinking motion with both hands, or can he or she only do one hand at a time?

If difficult, help guide the student through the motor action. Emphasize playing on the playground equipment and jumping activities.

Bilateral Integration

- Can the student move his or her arms together smoothly when waving streamers, or can only one arm at a time be moved?
- Can the student hold onto the hoop and rotate it, or does he or she just move the hoop to the right and then to the left?

If difficult, guide the student through the motor action. Slow the song down and have the student wave beanbags instead of streamers for more awareness of his or her hands.

Coordinating Both Sides of the Body

- Can the student hold onto a film container with one hand while releasing each penny into the container with the other hand?

If difficult, work on two-handed activities including stringing beads and rolling clay.

Auditory Processing

- Can the student sing "beep" into the kazoo at the correct time?

If difficult, emphasize rhythm and clapping games and songs.

Fine Motor

- Can the student touch his or her thumb to index and middle fingers during the blinking motion?

If student is unable to do this comfortably, practice finger plays and stringing beads.

- Can the student hold a penny in one hand while releasing another penny with the same hand into the film container, or do the pennies fall out of the student's hand?

If student is unable to complete the activity with one hand, do pegboard activities and fingerplays.

Crossing Midline

- Can the student cross the midline while waving streamers and when turning a hoop, or does the right hand stay on the right side of the body and the left hand remain on the left side?

If difficult, practice turning a jumprope, playing Simon Says, and doing clapping games.

Zoo Day

Materials

- 1 piece of recycled paper or newspaper per student
- 1 large piece of gray construction paper
- 1 beanbag per student
- masking tape
- stapler
- coffee can (optional)

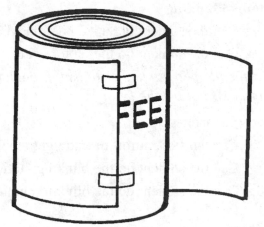

Teacher Preparation

1. Form gray construction paper into a cylinder, stapling at both ends. This will be the elephant's trunk. Try wrapping the construction paper around an empty coffee can for more stability.
2. Mark a trail on the floor, using masking tape. The trail can be straight or curved.

Directions to Students

Monkey See, Monkey Do

1. Today we are going to pretend we are animals at the zoo.
2. Our first animal will be a monkey. Follow along. Once we get started, there will be no talking, just moving.
3. Stand up and we'll form a circle (or a semi-circle or a line).
4. What are some movements a monkey might do? Let's jump up and down like a monkey. Can you howl like a monkey while scratching your tummy? (Other motions might be to clap hands, pat stomach, scratch head, or clap hands above head, etc.)

Monkey Walk

1. We are now going to walk on this line (point to the "trail" line you made using masking tape) like a monkey.
2. Place your hands and feet on the floor with your knees slightly bent. Walk along the trail.

Bear Walk

1. Now, let's walk like a bear.
2. Place your hands and feet on the floor, moving your right arm and leg together and then move your left arm and leg together. Walk along the trail.
3. Now try to walk like a bear with a beanbag on your back.

Monkey Faces

1. Let's make monkey faces. Watch me and imitate my facial expressions. (Make different facial expressions. Examples include wrinkling up nose, blowing air in both cheeks, putting air in right cheek and then switching to left cheek, blinking eyes, opening mouth wide, sticking out lower lip, raising eyebrows, smiling, clicking tongue, etc.)
2. Who would like to take a turn being the leader monkey?

14

Zoo Day *(cont.)*

Directions to Student *(cont.)*

Feed the Elephant

1. Do you see the gray cylinder standing upright on the floor? Lie on your stomachs, about 3' (.9 m) away from the cylinder.
2. Now feed the elephant peanuts. Imagine that the gray cylinder is the elephant's trunk. Lie down on your stomach so your head is facing the elephant's trunk.
3. Each of you has been given one piece of paper. Rip off small pieces of paper, about 2" x 4" (5 cm x 10 cm). Crumple these pieces of paper to make pretend peanuts.
4. After you have your peanuts, toss them into the elephant's trunk. Stay on your stomach, and if your peanut misses, that is okay. Keep trying.

Teacher note: If students are fairly accurate tossing the "peanuts," scoot them back so they have to throw farther.

Additional Activities

1. Students can take turns being monkeys and having their classmates imitate them.
2. Instead of doing a regular monkey walk, do a monkey hop with knees slightly bent. Have one hand on the head and the other hand patting the stomach.
3. Do the bear walk with a beanbag on the student's back. Don't let the bag slide off.
4. Have students squish the paper in one hand to make peanuts, or with one piece of paper in each hand.
5. Throw peanuts with the right hand, the left hand, or both hands at the same time.
6. Read a book about the zoo or about animals that might be seen in the zoo.

Observations for Sensory Motor Activities

Motor Planning

- Can the student follow the motor action of adults quickly, or is there a delay while figuring out how to do the motor action? Can student come up with different motor actions as the leader, or do they do the same motor actions as the student before them?
- Can the student do the bear walk while balancing a beanbag or does it continually fall off?
- Can the student throw peanuts into the elephant's trunk, or does he or she continually under- or overthrow?

If difficult, give directions at a slower pace and motor students through the activity.

Bilateral Integration

- Can the student do the bear walk, or does he or she move the right hand with the left leg and the left hand with the right leg?
- Can the student throw peanuts with both hands at the same time, or can he or she only throw with one hand at a time?

If difficult, practice playing Simon Says, jumping rope, and doing other two-handed activities.

Fine Motor

- Can the student rip small pieces of paper, or is the paper size too large or too small?

If difficult, have the student do more play dough activities, and encourage play with small manipulatives.

Head, Shoulders, Knees, and Toes

Materials

- 1 large sheet of paper (large enough for one student to lie down on)
- 1 small paint roller or paintbrush per student
- 10 stickers per student
- felt pen

Teacher Preparation

Lay out the long sheet of paper.

Directions to Students

Head, Shoulders, Knees, and Toes

Head, shoulders, knees, and toes, knees and toes.
Head, shoulders, knees, and toes, knees and toes.
Eyes and ears and mouth and nose,
Head, shoulders, knees, and toes.

1. Everyone stand up to sing the song.
2. We are going to sing it again and this time we are going to do the motor actions.
3. That was wonderful! I am going to give each of you a paintbrush or a paint roller. Hold the brush or roller in your hand.
4. This time we are going to sing the song slower and as we sing the different body parts, you need to paint that body part by rolling the paint roller or painting with the paintbrush on the appropriate spot. Practice rolling it or painting on your leg.
5. Great! Now we are going to sing the song as we brush using the paintbrush or roller.
6. Should we try it again? faster? Can you use your other hand to do the painting?

Outline of Body

1. Let's trace around one student and then hang the tracing up on the wall.
2. Who wants to be traced? (Select one student.) Great! Lie down on your back on the paper.
3. Tell me what body part is being traced, as the felt pen goes around this student's body.
4. Let's hang it on the wall. (Hang it within students' reach.)

Stickers and Body Parts

1. Each of you is going to receive 10 stickers. Do not touch the stickers until I tell you to pick them up.
2. Take one sticker and place it on your left shoulder. Take another sticker and place it on your right knee. Take one sticker and place it on your left toe, one sticker on your head, one sticker on your left ear. (Continue until all stickers are gone.)
3. That was wonderful. Now we are going to take turns putting stickers on the body tracing on the wall. Put one sticker on the body part called out.

Head, Shoulders, Knees, and Toes *(cont.)*

Additional Activities

1. Trace around each student on butcher paper.

2. Trace around each student's body on the playground, using chalk.

3. Have students draw their own bodies, using chalk on the playground.

4. Have student hold a paintbrush in his or her right hand and brush body parts on the left side of his or her body.

5. Hold a paintbrush in the left hand and brush body parts on the right side of the body.

6. Use different colored stickers and call out colors as well as what body part to stick the sticker on.

7. Have the student take all the stickers off and put them on the same body part on the paper outline of his or her body.

Observations for Sensory Motor Activities

Crossing Midline

- Can the student cross hand over the midline and paint the opposite side of his or her body with a paintbrush?
- Can the student cross over the midline to put stickers on body parts, or is the same hand used for the same side?

If difficult, encourage clapping games and chalkboard activities.

Motor Planning

- Can the student follow the motions for the songs, or does he or she need to watch others?

If difficult, slow down songs and motions.

Bilateral Integration

- Can the student do body actions with both hands, or can he or she only use one hand at a time?

If difficult, encourage more two-handed activities.

Fine Motor

- Can the student place stickers on one at a time and then take them off without ripping them?

If difficult, encourage stringing activities and work with manipulatives.

Dress-Up

Materials

- 2 pairs of baggy shorts with elastic waistbands (large enough to fit over the students' regular clothes)
- 2 large button-up shirts with the sleeves cut off (large enough to fit over the students' regular clothes)
- 1 board, approximately 18" x 24" (46 cm x 61 cm), of Plexiglas or plywood, or a cookie sheet
- 1 package each of red, yellow, and blue seam binding
- 1 package of ¹/₂" (1.3 cm) elastic
- sewing machine or needle and thread
- sticky-back Velcro®
- paper dolls (page 20) and clothes (page 21)
- masking tape
- scissors

Teacher Preparation

1. Cut blue, yellow, and red seam binding into approximately 7" (18 cm) long strips to make wristbands to fit students. Cut the elastic into 2" (5 cm) long strips.
2. Sew ¹/₂" (1.3 cm) elastic on both ends of the colored seam binding strips to make wristbands. Each student should have one band of each of the three colors.
3. Color, cut out, and laminate paper dolls and clothing patterns. Place small pieces of sticky-back Velcro on the fronts of the dolls as well as on the backs of the clothing.
4. A board of some kind at least 2' (61 cm) square is needed to hold the paper dolls.
5. Place sticky-back Velcro® on the paper dolls and paper doll clothes, as well as in two places on the board to hold the paper dolls.
6. Place masking tape on the floor, marking two trails for students to walk on. Trails can be straight, curved, or zigzag.
7. Place one pair of shorts and one shirt at one end of each trail.
8. Have paper dolls, clothing, and board close at hand.
9. Have wristbands nearby in sets of one red, one blue, and one yellow.

Directions to Students

Dress Up

1. Today we are going to play dress-up. Five students line up behind this trail (point to one trail), and five more stand in a line behind this trail (point to the other trail).
2. This is not a race. It does not make any difference who finishes first. We will continue until everyone has had a chance.
3. The first student in line needs to put on the shorts and the shirt and walk on the trail, heel-to-toe. Stay on the trail. When you get to the end of the trail, walk backwards heel-to-toe. Then take the shorts and the shirt off and give them to the next student to put on and walk the trail.

Dress-Up *(cont.)*

Directions to Students *(cont.)*

Dress-Up Paper Dolls

1. Did everyone have a turn playing the Dress-Up game? (Pick up the board that has the boy and girl paper dolls attached onto it by Velcro®. Sit in a chair at the end of the trails. Hold board at your knee level. Place paper doll clothing at students' end of the trail.)
2. We are going to play a different kind of dress-up game now. Form two lines again. Two at a time, pick up one piece of paper doll clothing in each hand and crawl on one of the trails to the paper dolls on the board. When you reach the board, lie down on your stomach. Reach up with both arms at the same time, and place the correct clothing on the paper dolls. Then, remove the paper clothing, and take it back to the next student in line at the beginning of the trail.

Wristbands

1. Get a red, blue, and yellow wrist band. Listen carefully to the directions.
2. Put the red wrist band on your right arm (pause), now a blue band (pause), and now a yellow band.
3. Take off the red wrist band (pause), now the blue band (pause), and now the yellow band.
4. Now put the blue wrist band on your left arm (pause), put the yellow band on your right arm (pause), and put the red band on your left arm (pause). Take off the yellow band, then the red band, and then the blue band.

Additional Activity

Have students alternate jumping to the right and to the left of the trail, etc. Have students walk on the trail on their heels or on their toes. Have students crawl on their bellies on the trail.

Observations for Sensory Motor Activities

Motor Planning

- Can the student put on the oversized shorts and shirt, or is help needed? Can the student put clothing on while standing, or does he or she need to sit down?

If difficult, give the student visual or physical prompts.

Body Awareness

- Can the student put wristbands on following verbal directions, or does he or she not know right from left?

If the student confuses left and right, emphasize only left or only right when using the wristbands until the student knows left and right.

Bilateral

- While lying on his or her tummy, can the student hold one piece of paper clothing in each hand, lift arms up, and place the clothing correctly on the paper dolls, or does he or she roll to one side and only lift one arm up at a time?

If difficult, emphasize two-handed activities.

Fine Motor

- Can the student button buttons on a dress shirt? Can the student use both hands when putting wristbands on and taking them off?

If difficult, work on stringing activities.

Dress-Up (cont.)

Paper Doll Patterns

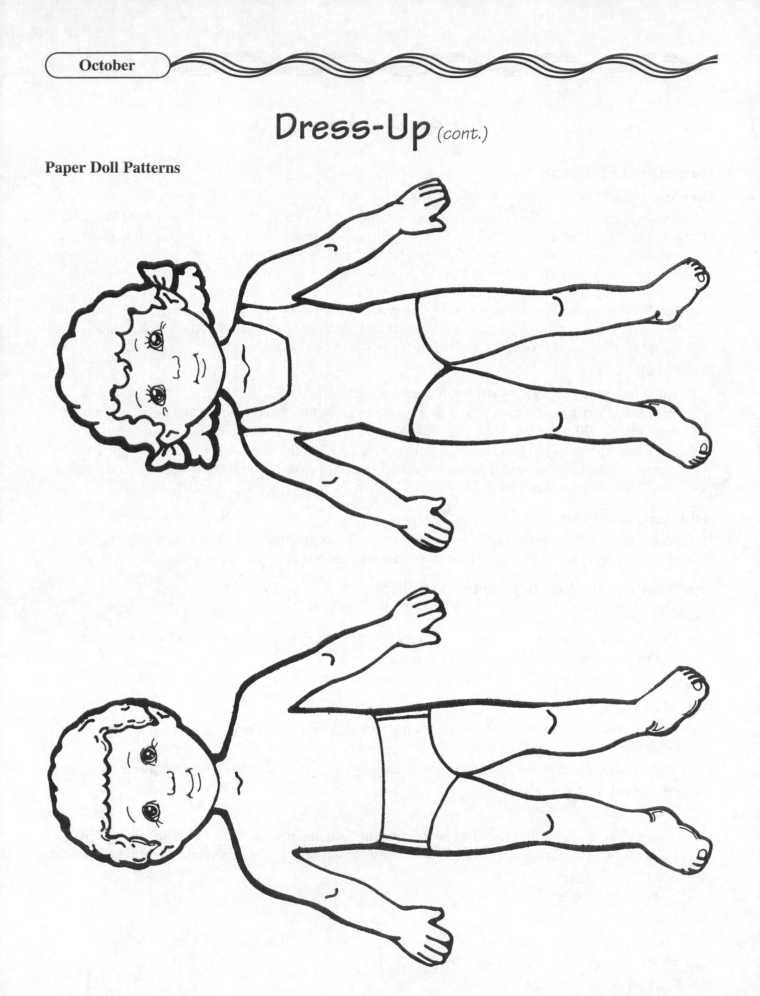

Dress-Up (cont.)

Fall Clothes Patterns

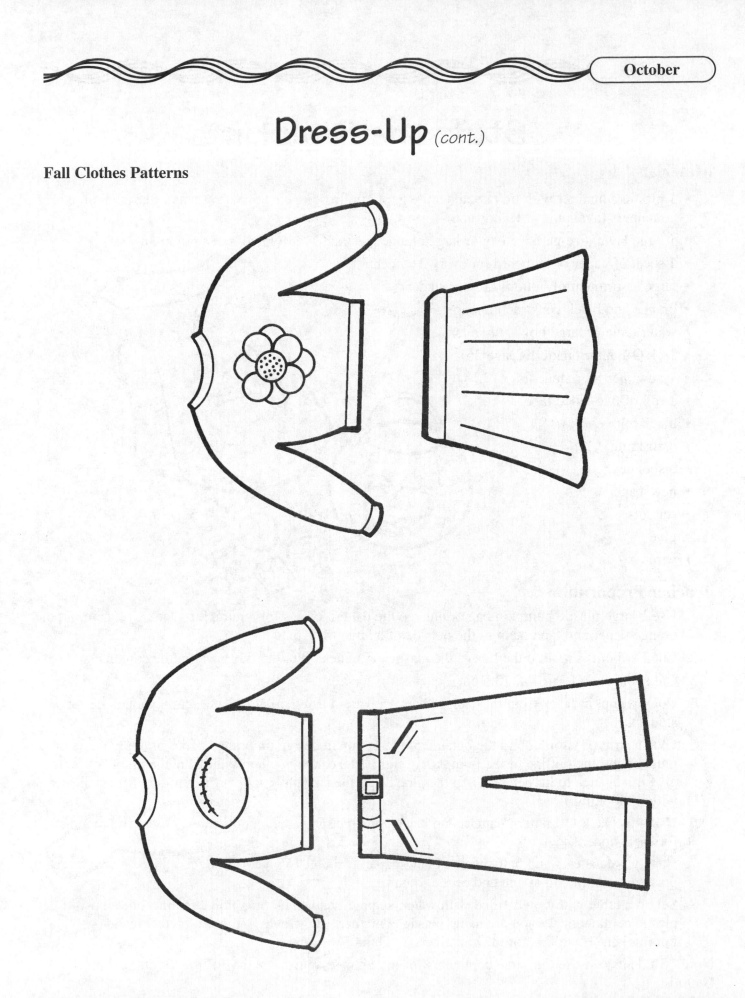

Stuff the Pumpkin

Materials

- 1 plastic container with lid per student (e.g. plastic frosting containers) or small plastic, pumpkin containers (available at Halloween)
- 1 large lawn-size garbage bag or large orange plastic bag decorated like a pumpkin
- 1 sheet of paper or tagboard for every 2 students
- large assortment of buttons (12 per student)
- orange and black construction paper
- water table or large bowls of water
- Jack O'Lantern pattern (page 26)
- 1 bowl per four students
- 1 roll of two-sided tape
- black felt pen
- craft knife
- 3 sponges
- newspaper
- scissors
- glue
- yarn

Teacher Preparation

1. Use a large plastic pumpkin bag or enlarge the pattern pieces for a pumpkin face. Cut them out of orange paper and tape them to the outside of a large trash bag.
2. Cut 2" (5 cm) slits into the lids of the plastic containers. Put the lids back on the containers.
3. Cut sponges to form 1½" (3.5 cm) squares.
4. Copy pumpkin faces from the Jack O'Lantern pattern using orange construction paper, one set per student.
5. Glue a strip of yarn around the outside of the pumpkin design on orange paper or apply a line of glue around the outline of the pumpkin design. Make sure you apply the glue the night before to give it a chance to harden. (When the glue dries, the students can feel the outline of the pumpkin without looking.)
6. Using the Jack O'Lantern pattern and black construction paper, cut out eyes, noses, and mouths for each student.
7. Have whole sheets and half sheets of newspaper available to give to students. Place a large plastic pumpkin bag at one end of the room.
8. Set up a table with bowls filled with water, sponges, and small pumpkin containers or empty plastic containers. If you are using plastic containers, draw pumpkin faces on the outside using a felt marker. Have lids for the containers and buttons nearby.

Note: Students can use the same containers for the Sponge Squeeze and Stuff the Pumpkin with Buttons.

Stuff the Pumpkin *(cont.)*

Directions to Students

Stuff the Pumpkin

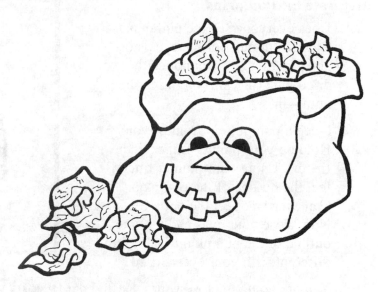

1. Today we are going to stuff the pumpkin. Everyone pick up one sheet of newspaper. Using both your hands, crumble the paper into a small, tight ball. Squeeze it as tightly as you can.

2. Put the newspaper ball down and pick up another sheet of newspaper. Crumble it up into another small ball. Now you have two small balls of newspaper.

3. Hold one ball in each hand. Crawl to the plastic pumpkin bag on the other side of the classroom. When you reach the pumpkin bag, throw the balls in, and crawl back to where you were sitting.

4. Continue taking turns until the bag is full and looks like a stuffed pumpkin.

5. Look at the pumpkin; it looks so big! Great job stuffing it!

Sponge Squeeze

1. Let's stuff our little pumpkins (or plastic containers) with water at the water table.

2. Get a small pumpkin container and a sponge.

3. Put your sponge in the water, get it full of water, and then squeeze it into your pumpkin container. Squeeze with just one hand and squeeze really hard. Try to use all your fingers and thumb to squeeze, and squeeze until the sponge is practically dry.

4. Continue getting your sponge wet and squeezing it into your container. (If containers are small, students can fill them. If containers are large, have students squeeze the sponges about ten times.)

5. When you are finished "stuffing" your pumpkin container, carefully pour the water from your pumpkin back into the water bowl or water table.

Stuff the Pumpkin with Buttons

1. Sit down next to a pumpkin container and a bowl of buttons. Make sure the lid is securely on the container. Take some time to examine the buttons.

2. This time, stuff the pumpkins with buttons. Pick up three buttons in one hand. Use only one hand. Now put the buttons, one at a time, into the slit cut in the lid of the container. Remember, use only one hand. Continue until all the buttons have been "stuffed" in a pumpkin.

Note: Each student should have the opportunity to put in at least 12 buttons.

Stuff the Pumpkin *(cont.)*

Directions to Students *(cont.)*

Decorate the Pumpkins

1. Does everyone see the pumpkins and the cut outs for the eyes, nose, and mouth? Did you notice the dried glue (or yarn) outlining the pumpkin?

2. Place a pumpkin in front of you. Hold up your pointer finger (index finger). Using your pointer finger, feel the outline of the pumpkin. Can everyone feel the outline? Now close your eyes and feel the outline of the pumpkin. Did it feel different with your eyes closed?

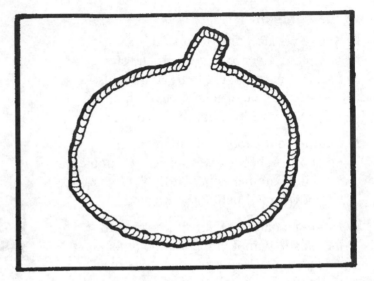

3. You are going to close your eyes and put faces on your pumpkins. I wonder what our pumpkins will look like. Work with a partner. One student will put the face on the pumpkin while the partner is holding a piece of tagboard under his or her chin so he or she cannot see the pumpkin picture.

4. Let's have one partner pick up the tagboard and place it under the other's chin. Make sure the pumpkin has two eyes, one nose, and one mouth on it, and that there is glue (or two-sided tape) on each piece.

5. While one partner is holding the tagboard, the other partner will begin making the face.

6. The student who is making the face picks up one piece at a time, feels the glue outline of the pumpkin with his or her finger, and puts the piece where he or she thinks it belongs. Continue until the pumpkin face is complete. Don't look until it is finished.

7. After one partner finishes, trade places and let the other make the pumpkin face.

Later, have a discussion with the students. Compliment their work, and ask if it was hard to make the faces without looking. Ask who wanted to look. Compliment the group for being so creative at using their hands and sense of touch.

Stuff the Pumpkin *(cont.)*

Additional Activities

1. Use different weights of paper including tissue paper, construction paper, wax paper, tagboard, etc., to crumble up and stuff in the bag pumpkin.

2. Have students hold a half of a newspaper sheet in each hand and crumble them both up using only that hand.

3. Crawl around obstacles, such as desks or chairs, and crawl over bolsters or small rolls or mats to get to the pumpkin trash bags.

4. When squeezing sponges, have the students use only their right hand or their left hand, not both together.

5. Have students squeeze paper or sponges using their thumbs and all fingers and then just using their thumbs, index, and middle fingers.

6. Have students put the outlines of glue and/or yarn on their own pumpkins the day before the Decorate the Pumpkins activity.

7. Have students cut out eyes, noses, and mouths for their pumpkin faces.

Observations for Sensory Motor Activities

Motor Planning

- Can the student crawl when holding a newspaper ball in each hand, or does he or she crawl on his or her elbows?

- Can the student squeeze newspaper or a sponge just using one hand, or are both hands used?

- Can the student manipulate buttons in one hand, or is the other hand nessessary to assist in moving buttons?

If difficult, give slower, less detailed directions and guide student through the activity.

Body Awareness

- Can the student glue pumpkin face pieces on without looking at what his or her hands are doing?

Some children need to look at their hands to know what their hands are doing. If difficult, do heavy work activities like jumping, jungle gym, and crawling activities.

Fine Motor

- Can the student squeeze the sponges until all the water is gone?

- Can the student squeeze with one hand, or are two hands needed?

- Can the student squeeze water into the container, or does it spill?

- Can the student pick up paper face pieces and put them on the pumpkin without looking?

- Can the student manipulate face pieces so the pumpkin face looks fairly accurate, or are the pieces placed inaccurately?

If difficult, practice stringing activities and play with play dough.

Stuff the Pumpkin *(cont.)*

Jack O'Lantern

26

Haunted House

Materials

- 20 small plastic Halloween objects, such as rings, spiders, etc.
- 4 door mats or bath mats with different textures
- 1 package cooked, cold spaghetti
- 4 large bowls or pans
- 2 yards of fabric
- 1 box cornstarch
- 5' (152 cm) bubble paper
- masking tape
- 1 pumpkin
- 1 blanket
- scissors
- knife
- table

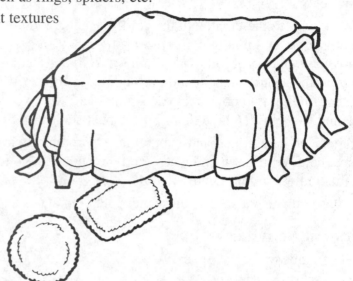

Teacher Preparation

1. Cut the fabric into two one-yard (.9 m) sections. Cut the fabric into 2" (5 cm) wide streamers, leaving one side connected. (See illustration above.)
2. Attach the fabric streamers at either end of the table using tape so the streamers touch the floor.
3. Place bubble paper and the different mats under the table for students to crawl on.
4. Cover the table with a blanket just to make it darker, like a haunted house.
5. Cook the spaghetti the night before and put the cold spaghetti in a pan. Hide several of the plastic objects inside.
6. Mix cornstarch and water until it has a runny consistency. Place several plastic Halloween objects in the mixture.
7. Cut the top off the pumpkin and place several plastic Halloween objects inside the pumpkin, mixed in with the pumpkin seeds.
8. Place different mats, bubble paper, or other different textured items in a line leading to the Haunted House (table).
9. Place pans of cold spaghetti, cornstarch and water, and the pumpkin on a table.

Directions to Students

Haunted House

1. It is Haunted House Day.
2. First, take off your shoes and socks and place them behind you.

    Teacher note: Taking shoes and socks off is time consuming, but it allows an opportunity to see which students have difficulty and may need more assistance with fine motor, self-care activities.

3. When you are barefoot, walk on the path one at a time to the Haunted House (covered table), and then crawl through it.

Haunted House *(cont.)*

Directions to Students *(cont.)*

Creepy Feely

1. Walk over to the table with the cold spaghetti, and the cornstarch, and pumpkin mixtures. In each of these, there are some plastic objects that you need to find. (Demonstrate by putting your hands in and pulling out one object.) Take turns finding two objects in each container. After you have found two objects, hide them for the next student to find.

2. After you have found and then replaced two objects in the spaghetti, cornstarch and water, and the pumpkin, go to the sink and wash your hands.

3. After you wash and dry your hands, put your shoes and socks back on.

Additional Activities

1. Play a tape or record of scary music.
2. Turn the lights down in the classroom.
3. Have students make scary haunting sounds.
4. Have more pans filled with different tactile mediums such as peeled grapes, dried beans, etc.
5. Walk on the path to the Haunted House on tip toes, heels, hands and knees, hands and feet, or by rolling.
6. Hang spiders or wind socks under the Haunted House.

Observations for Sensory Motor Activities

Tactile

- Can the student walk and crawl on the different textures, or does he or she resist?
- Can the student go through hanging fabric, or is there hesitation?
- Can the student put his or her hands into the many tactile mediums, or are fingertips used to pull objects out?

Hands and feet are the most sensitive if students are tactile defensive. If difficult, encourage but don't insist.

Fine Motor

- Can the student wash his or her hands using a back and forth motion, or does the student just let the water run over his or her hands?
- Can the student use his or her hands to take shoes and socks off, or are shoes kicked off?
- Can the student turn socks the correct way to put them on, or is the sock put on upside down?
- Can the student tie a knot and a bow, or does he or she have no idea where to start?

Encourage hand washing in a back and forth motion and putting on hand lotion. Use play dough, pegboards, and small manipulatives.

Trick or Treat

Materials

- large beanbag chair or 2 yards (182 cm) fabric and foam, old towels etc., for filling
- 1 bottle of bubbles and wand per pair of students
- 1 large playground ball or therapy ball (See resources.)
- at least 3 stickers (stars, colored dots) per student
- large wooden block (big enough to stand on)
- enlarged, laminated clown pattern (page 31)
- candy, stickers, or Halloween treats
- 1 pinwheel per pair of students
- plastic pumpkin container
- sewing machine
- 4 beanbags
- scissors

Teacher Preparation

1. If you don't have a large beanbag, you can make a large pillow. Lay out a piece of material that is 2 yards (182 cm) long and approximately 36" (91 cm) across. Place the two ends together and pin. Pin the other two sides. Now sew a straight seam about $\frac{1}{2}$" (1.3 cm) around two and one half sides, leaving an opening of at least 12" (30 cm). Remove the pins. Turn the material inside out and stuff it with foam, old towels, or smaller soft pillows.

2. Enlarge the clown pattern and laminate it.

3. If you don't have a pumpkin container, you can make one by covering a box with orange construction paper and adding black construction paper eyes, nose, and mouth to one side of the box.

4. Place the beanbag chair or large pillow on the floor with the wooden block in front of it.

Directions to Students

Over, Under, and On

1. Has everyone been trick-or-treating? Today all you need to do is a few tricks before you get your treat.

2. Line up behind this wooden block. First, jump off the box and land on the beanbag. After you jump, walk to the end of the line.

3. Next, crawl over the beanbag. Then, crawl under the beanbag. Finally, crawl around the beanbag. Can anyone think of another trick you can do on the beanbag pillow?

Beanbags in Pumpkin

1. Does everyone see the wooden block? (Place it approximately 5' [152 cm] from the pumpkin container. Distance depends on the age of the students and how well they can throw.) There are four beanbags next to the wooden block.

Trick or Treat *(cont.)*

Directions to Students *(cont.)*

Beanbags in Pumpkin *(cont,)*

2. Stand on the block, reach down, and pick up one beanbag. Stand up and throw the beanbag at the pumpkin. Try to stay on the block. After you have thrown four beanbags, retrieve them and replace them for the next student.

Blowing Activities

1. Lie down on the floor on your stomachs. Do you see the toys on the floor? How do these toys work? (Have bubbles and pinwheels or other blow toys within reach.)
2. Today, we are going to see how long you can blow bubbles and pinwheels while you are on your stomach. Find a partner. One of you should have bubbles, and the other should have a pinwheel.
3. See if you can blow for the count of five. 1, 2, 3, 4, 5. (If all students can do this, try counting to 10.)
4. Trade toys and try blowing to a count of five again.

Decorate the Clown

1. Do you see the big ball in front of the clown picture? (Hold the clown picture up or hang it on the wall at students' shoulder level.) There are some stickers on the floor by the ball, too.
2. This clown needs to be decorated. He looks so dull. Sit on the ball, reach down, pick up one sticker at a time, and place it on the clown. Place three stickers on the clown.

Additional Activities

1. Have students reach to the right and left when sitting on the ball for stickers to put on the clown.
2. Have students put small beanbags on their heads or shoulders and knee-walk around the pumpkin.
3. Instead of putting stickers on the clown, have students use a crayon to draw a circle, square, triangle, or star on the named clown body part.

Observations for Sensory Motor Activities

Motor Planning

- Can the student go over and under the beanbag pillow, or does he or she get stuck and not know what to do?
- Can the student sit on the ball, bend over to pick up stickers, and reach up to put the stickers on the clown, or does he or she fall off the ball? Can the student stand on the wooden block and throw beanbags, or does he or she lose his or her balance?

If difficult, encourage jumping, hopping, and skipping activities.

Body Awareness

- Can the student correctly put stickers on named body parts of the clown?

If difficult, practice playing Simon Says.

- Can the student blow hard enough to make the pinwheel spin or are breaths short and not strong?

If difficult, have students practice blowing cotton balls or Ping-Pong balls across tables or the floor.

Fine Motor

- Can the student peel stickers off the backing, or does he or she crumple the paper?

To develop more muscle strength in fingers, encourage fingerplays and stringing activities.

Trick or Treat(cont.)

Clown Pattern

Falling Leaves

Materials

- green, brown, yellow, and red construction paper
- 20–40 leaves (real, silk, or plastic)
- 1 sheet of white paper per student
- 4 brooms (child- or adult-sized)
- 6 bricks or large cans of food
- 2 sturdy cardboard boxes
- masking tape
- 12" (30 cm) rope
- peeled crayons

Teacher Preparation

1. Collect leaves or use leaves from silk and plastic flowers.

2. Using a sturdy cardboard box (any size), punch a hole in one side about 4" (10 cm) down from the top of the box. Push the rope through this hole and tie a knot on the inside of the box so the rope does not pull through. The students will put the leaves in the box.

3. Place bricks or cans (for weight) in the bottom of the cardboard box. The number of bricks or food cans will depend on how much weight your students can pull.

4. Have paper, peeled crayons, and leaves on the table to do leaf rubbings.

5. Scatter leaves on the floor in a 5' (152 cm) square area.

6. Mark a trail on the floor using masking tape. The trail should be curved or zigzagged. Have the end of the trail stop close to beginning of the trail.

Note: Make two different trails if your group is large.

Directions to Students

Falling Leaves

1. Do any of you have trees by your homes that are losing their leaves? Let's all pretend we are falling leaves.

2. Stand up tall on your tip toes with your arms way above your head. Let yourself fall like a leaf to the ground. Some of you fell fast and landed hard and some of you drifted through the air and took a long time to reach the floor.

3. Let's all be heavy leaves. How would a heavy leaf fall to the ground? Now, let's be lighter leaves being blown in a slight breeze. How might we move?

4. How else might a leaf fall to the ground?

Falling Leaves *(cont.)*

Directions to Students *(cont.)*

Sweeping the Leaves

1. Do you see all the leaves on the ground (floor)? Let's take turns sweeping the leaves into a pile and putting them into a container.

2. Work in groups of four to sweep the leaves into one pile. When you sweep, you need to hold the broom with two hands and sweep in front of you.

3. As soon as the leaves are in a neat pile, pick them up and put them into a cardboard box.

4. Take turns pulling the box full of leaves (and weighted down with cans or bricks) along the trail to the compost pile.

5. Try not to go off the line. When you get to the end of your trail, dump out the leaves for the next group.

   Note: Have the trail end near the beginning of the line so the student can dump the leaves out at the compost pile and the next group of students can start sweeping up the leaves.

Wheelbarrow

1. Sometimes we use wheelbarrows to carry dried leaves. Has anyone seen a wheelbarrow being used? We are going to become wheelbarrows. Everyone find a partner.

2. One student needs to get down on hands and knees. The partner will pick up the first student's legs and rest them on his or her hips. (Depending on the age of your students, they may need to be held at the knees or ankles. The younger the child, the less arm strength they have, so they need to be held at the knees for more support.)

3. Pick up your partner's legs and move forward on the line. Wonderful job! Everyone certainly worked hard.

Leaf Rubbings

1. Now we are going to do leaf rubbings. Choose a good, veined leaf and tape the stem to the table.

2. Place a piece of paper over the leaf and smooth it down with your hand.

3. Pick up your crayon and hold it on its side. Carefully rub the crayon back and forth across the paper. Can you see the imprint of the leaf?

Falling Leaves (cont.)

Additional Activities

1. Have three boxes: one for students to pull by rope, one for students to push, and last box for the students to pull.

2. Have students sweep leaves into a dust pan before putting them into the box.

3. Read a book about falling leaves. Try *Autumn Leaves* by Ken Robbins, Scholastic, 1998.

4. Take a walk around the school or the playground looking for dried, fallen leaves. Gather them up, crumple them into a box and use them in the compost pile, or mix them into the soil, or use them as ground cover.

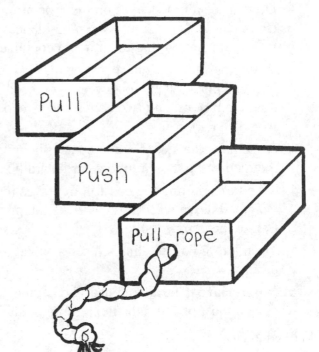

Observations for Sensory Motor Activities

Bilateral Integration

- Can the student hold the broom using both hands and sweep across the front of the body, or is only one hand used?

- Can the student sweep in front of self, or does he or she sweep off to the side?

If difficult, work on two-handed activities.

Body Awareness

- Can student stand up tall and fall slowly with good body control when pretending he or she is a falling leaf, or are his or her arm movements jerky?

If difficult, do activities like Simon Says.

Motor Planning

- Can the student pull or push a heavy box and stay on the line, or does he or she fall down and go off the line?

If difficult, practice carrying heavy objects.

Fine Motor

- Can the student hold a crayon and rub it across paper while holding the paper with the other hand, or does he or she just use one hand?

If difficult, practice tracing around different objects.

34

Car Wash

Materials

- 1 or more empty plastic containers with plastic lids (Empty film or frosting containers work well.)
- 3 empty tennis ball containers with lids
- 1 scooter board or skateboard (See resources.)
- 5–6' (152–182 cm) clothesline
- 4 washcloths or small towels
- 4 winged clothespins
- 2 large, soft sponges
- 20 or more pennies
- 2 carpet squares
- 7' (2 m) rope
- 2 chairs
- scissors
- cardboard building blocks (optional)

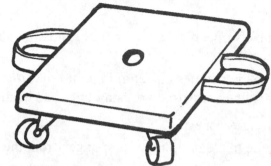

Teacher Preparation

1. Cut a 1" (2.54 cm) slit into the lid of an empty plastic container. Put the lid back on the container.
2. Cut 1" (2.54 cm) diameter circles in the middle of the lids from the empty tennis ball containers. Replace the lids.
3. Make winged clothespins. (Directions are on page 8)
4. Cut soft sponges into approximately 1" (2.54 cm) cubes.
5. Attach the clothesline between the tops of two chairs. Place the washcloths and winged clothespins under the clothesline.
6. Attach the rope to a door handle or the leg of a heavy desk. Place two carpet squares at the unattached end of the rope along with a scooter board.

Note: Since students will be pulling on the rope, the place of attachment needs to be sturdy.

Directions to Students

Car Wash

1. Today we are going to wash our cars.
2. Lie on your stomach on a scooter board. Grab the rope and pull hard, hand over hand, to the end of the rope. Make sure to use your arms, not your feet.
3. As you pull yourself along, the carpet squares will be gently flapped on you like the flappers at the car wash. (As students pull themselves across the floor, an adult holds one carpet square in each hand and flaps them on the student.)

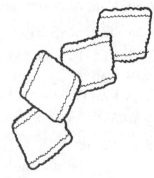

4. After you finish the car wash, imagine you are all wet. You'll need to get a towel from the clothesline and dry yourself off.
5. Dry your arms, legs, stomach, and back with the towel.
6. Wring out your towel and hang it back up on clothesline using the winged clothespins.

Note: If you don't have a scooter board, have students crawl on a line or have students lie on their stomachs and pull on the rope with their arms.

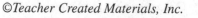

Car Wash *(cont.)*

Directions to Students *(cont.)*

Pay for Car Wash

1. Now that you have gone through the car wash, you need to pay.

2. Pick up five pennies, one at a time, and hold all five in your hand.

3. Release the pennies one at a time into the slit on top of the container. Try to do it using only one hand.

Putting Sponges Away

1. It is time to clean-up the wet sponges from the car wash.

2. Pick up one sponge, squeeze it hard, and then pick up another. See if you can pick up five sponges and hold them all in one hand.

3. Put them one at a time into the tennis ball container.

Additional Activities

1. Go through an obstacle course on the way to the car wash. Travel between buildings (boxes), around trees (chairs), under bridges (tables), and through a tunnel (table covered with a blanket).

2. Have students name their body parts as they are drying them off.

3. Have students squeeze the towels with two hands and wring them out.

4. Present three colors of sponges and three empty tennis ball containers with holes in the lids. The tennis ball containers should be covered with paper matching the colors of the sponges. Have students place the colored sponges into the matching color containers.

Observations for Sensory Motor Activities

Motor Planning

- Can the student crawl or scoot on a scooter board around obstacles without bumping into items?

If difficult, have the student slow down and give him or her visual cues.

Bilateral Integration

- Can the student pull hand-over-hand on the rope, or does he or she pull with the same hand?
- Can the student wring a towel out with both hands and twist it, or does he or she just squeeze the towel?

If difficult, work on two-handed activities.

Fine Motor

- Can the student hold more than two sponges in one hand at a time and release them one at a time, or can only one sponge be manipulated at a time?

If difficult, continue to work on student's picking up two objects and holding them in one hand.

36

Leaves

Materials

- brown, yellow, green, and red construction paper
- 20–30 real, fallen leaves
- 1 scarf per student
- 1 beanbag per student
- bowl of uncooked rice
- 2 boxes, same size
- play dough
- glue

Teacher Preparation

1. Cut out several leaves using brown, yellow, red, and green construction paper. Make at least one leaf per student.
2. Place several real dried leaves into each of the two boxes. There should be about the same amount of leaves in each box.
3. Have an assortment of scarves and/or beanbags for students to throw up in the air and catch.
4. Have rice, glue, and play dough ready for students to use.
5. Have paper leaves ready to place on the floor.

Directions to Students

Leaves in the Wind

1. We are going to pretend these scarves or beanbags are leaves that are blowing in the wind. Can you throw your scarf or beanbag up in the air and catch it with two hands? Everyone do that. Great! (Allow time for many throws.)
2. Now we are going to make it a little more difficult. See if you can do the following movements:
   - Toss the scarf or beanbag up in the air with one hand and catch it with the same hand.
   - Toss the scarf or beanbag up in the air with one hand and catch it with the opposite hand.
   - Toss the scarf or beanbag up in the air with your right hand and catch it with your left hand. Now throw the scarf or beanbag up with your left hand and catch it with your right hand. Did you know that this is how jugglers start learning to juggle?
   - Toss the scarf or beanbag up in the air and clap once before you catch it.
3. Can anyone think of another way we can throw and catch our scarves?

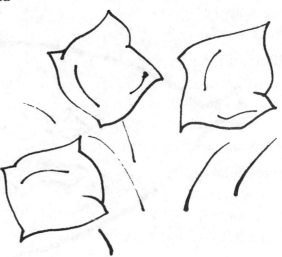

Leaves *(cont.)*

Directions to Students *(cont.)*

Beanbag Toss

1. Do you see the 10 paper leaves scattered on the floor? Let's count them. One, two, three . . . .

2. There are five beanbags in front of one of the leaves. Do you see them?

3. Let's have one student at a time stand on the leaf with the beanbags in front of it. Pick up one beanbag and throw it at the color of the leaf called out. Try to throw the beanbag right on top of the leaf.

4. When you have thrown the five beanbags, pick them up and place them in front of the leaf for the next student.

Crushing Leaves

1. There are two boxes filled with about the same number of leaves. What do you think would happen if we crushed the leaves in one box? Would the leaves take up as much room? Let's try.

2. Everyone can pick up one leaf from the same box, crumble it up, and return it to the same box. What happened? Were we right? Do the crushed leaves take up less space than the whole leaves in the other box?

Bugs on Leaves

1. On the table are paper leaves, glue, rice, and play dough. Pick up one paper leaf.

2. You are going to put bugs on your leaf. Put one drop of glue on the leaf, and then place one piece of rice in each drop of glue. Add four or five "bugs" to your leaf.

3. Now take a small piece of play dough about the size of a raisin and roll it between your hands to make a worm. (Demonstrate.) Place this worm on your leaf.

38

Leaves (cont.)

Additional Activities

1. Two students stand about five feet (152 cm) apart and toss one scarf or beanbag back and forth.

2. Two students stand about five feet (152 cm) apart, each holding a scarf or beanbag. On the count of three, students simultaneously toss scarves or beanbags at each other and catch the one thrown to them.

3. Have one student throw a beanbag to a partner and then do a pattern such as clap two times, jump one time. When the partner throws the beanbag back, he or she repeats the pattern.

4. Have students jump from leaf to leaf.

5. Have students cut out their own leaves from a pattern and decorate them.

6. Read *Red Leaf, Yellow Leaf* by Lois Ehlert, Harcourt Brace, 1991.

Observations for Sensory Motor Activities

Motor Planning

- Can the student toss a scarf or beanbag accurately to another student, or does he or she under- or overthrow?

If difficult, throw slowly. Try the activity using balloons.

- Can the student squeeze just one drop of glue out, or does the glue flow out?

If difficult, practice with eyedroppers, dropping one drop of water at a time, and practice picking up items using tweezers or tongs.

Bilateral Integration

- Can the student toss a scarf or beanbag with one hand and catch it with the other hand, or are two hands needed to catch it?

- Can the student catch the scarf in one or two hands, or do they back away when the scarf comes close?

- Can the student toss the scarf with one hand and catch it with the other?

If difficult, work on two-handed activities, and practice this activity with a balloon.

Fine Motor

- Can the student roll play dough into a worm using only his or her hands, or does he or she need to roll it on the table?

If difficult, have the student do more play dough activities.

- Can the student accurately place one grain of rice on a dab of glue?

If difficult, have the student pick up just one grain of rice at a time.

Turkey Trot

Materials

- orange, green, brown, and red tissue paper
- small box of unpopped popcorn
- 1 sheet of tagboard per student
- turkey pattern (page 42)
- glue or glue stick
- 7' (212 cm) rope per group of 6
- O-shaped cereal
- masking tape
- tennis ball per group of 6
- craft knife
- birdseed or grain
- scissors

Teacher Preparation

1. Copy and cut out one turkey pattern per student, using the tagboard.

2. Cut tissue paper into approximately 5" x 8" (13 cm x 20 cm) pieces.

3. Using a craft knife, cut an X into a tennis ball. The slits forming the X should be approximately 1" (2.54 cm) long.

4. Tie a knot in one end of the rope and push the knot through the X in the tennis ball. This makes the shot rope.

5. Arrange the tagboard turkeys, tissue paper, O-shaped cereal, and glue on a table.

Directions to Students

Turkey Trot

1. We are going to be turkeys today. Let's do the turkey trot.

2. Place your hands under your armpits and make your elbows go up and down. As you are walking say, "gobble, gobble, gobble."

3. Let's make one long line and do the turkey trot. We'll walk around the classroom, between the chairs, and under the table.

Jump the Shot Rope

1. Arrange yourselves in groups of five.

2. Stand and make a circle. One student is going to stand in the center of the circle and hold onto this rope at the end opposite the tennis ball.

3. When the student in the middle squats down and spins the rope, the rest of you in the circle need to jump over the shot (rope with ball attached to it) as it passes by you.

4. The student in the middle can turn five to six times and then switch positions.

Turkey Picture

1. Everyone is going to get a turkey picture to decorate. First, use the tissue paper.

2. Watch me. (Demonstrate.) Rip the tissue paper into small pieces about 2" (5 cm). Make sure when you rip the paper that your pieces are not too small or too big.

40

Turkey Trot *(cont.)*

Directions to Students *(cont.)*

Turkey Picture *(cont.)*

3. Place a dab of glue every place on the feathers where you want to put some tissue paper.
4. Crumble each piece of tissue paper up in your hand and place it on the feathers of the turkey.
5. Now, put dabs of glue on the turkey body. Place an O-shaped piece of cereal every place there is a dab of glue.

Turkey Feeding Time

1. It's turkey feeding time. Does anyone know what a turkey eats? Turkeys eat grain. We are going to pretend that our fingers are turkey beaks. The popcorn and birdseed will be our grain.
2. Imagine your hand is a turkey and your index and middle fingers are its head and beak. Let's wrap tape around each of your index and middle fingers so the sticky side is facing out.
3. Kneel down by the grain and move your taped hand along it. Start the turkey eating by getting grain on the front, back, and sides of your tape.
4. After your tape is full of grain you can take the tape off and throw it in the trash.

Additional Activities

1. Enlarge the turkey picture and have all the students work cooperatively on one picture.
2. Place the materials on the floor and hang the turkey pictures on the wall on the table so that the students continually need to bend down to pick up the tissue or O-shaped cereal and then stand up to place them on the picture.

Observations for Sensory Motor Activities

Motor Planning

- Can the student walk like a turkey, moving his or her arms and saying, "gobble, gobble" at the same time, or is only one movement at a time possible?

If difficult, start with one movement and then slowly incorporate more.

Bilateral Integration

- Can the student (with tape on his or her fingers) pick up bird seed and popcorn with both hands? Can the student cross the midline to pick up rice and popcorn?

If difficult, practice two-handed activities.

Tactile Awareness

- Can the student tolerate taped fingers, or is the tape taken off before picking up the grain?

If difficult, gently squeeze student's hand before putting tape on it or have the student rub his or her hands on the carpet.

Fine Motor

- Can the student tear adequate pieces of tissue paper, or are pieces too small or too big? Can the student pick up O-shaped cereal and place it on a dab of glue, or are several pieces picked up at a time?

If difficult, emphasize fingerplays and stringing activities.

Turkey Trot (cont.)

Turkey

Gingerbread Man

Materials

- gingerbread man cookie cutters or circle cookie cutters
- 2 cake decorating bags or empty condiment squeeze bottles
- 1 gingerbread man cookie or gingersnap cookie per student
- paper for copying patterns
- gingerbread man pattern (page 46)
- rolling pins or dowels
- 30–40 small pegs
- cookie sheet
- craft sticks
- play dough
- frosting
- scissors
- spatulas
- crayons
- raisins
- glue

Teacher Preparation

1. Copy one gingerbread man pattern per student. Make one class set of patterns, by enlarging the pictures on page 44. Include an old woman, an old man, one cow, one dog, one horse, and one fox.

2. Color the patterns, laminate them, and then glue them onto craft sticks in preparation for acting out the story.

3. Have play dough at the table. Arrange dowels or rolling pins, cookie cutters, pegs, and spatulas next to the play dough.

4. Place frosting in cake decorating bags or in empty condiment squeeze bottles. Have cookies, frosting, and raisins available at the table.

5. Place a cookie sheet on the opposite side of the room from where the students will be starting.

Directions to Students

The Story of the Gingerbread Man

1. We are going to act out the poem about the gingerbread man. Get a paper gingerbread man and stand in a circle. Hold your gingerbread man in your right hand.

2. As the poem is read, act out the movements of the gingerbread man. If he runs, run in place, if he crawls, crawl around the room. When it is time to roll, we will all go in the same direction. Be careful not to bump into your classmates. When it is time to hide from the fox, we will crawl under a table (or through a fabric tunnel). Is everyone ready?

Gingerbread Man *(cont.)*

Directions to Students *(cont.)*

Gingerbread Man

(Hold your gingerbread man up in the air.)

Run, run
As fast as you can.
You can't catch me,
I'm the Gingerbread Man!

(Hold up the old woman and the old man.)

Here come the old woman
And the old man.
Jump, jump, (in place)
As fast as you can.

(Hold up picture of a cow.)

Here comes a cow,
Mr. Gingerbread Man.
Crawl, crawl,
As fast as you can.

(Hold up picture of a dog.)

Here comes a dog,
Mr. Gingerbread Man.
Roll, roll,
As fast as you can.

(Hold up picture of a horse.)

Here comes a horse,
Mr. Gingerbread Man.
Gallop, gallop,
As fast as you can.

(Hold up picture of a fox and position yourself at the end of a table.)

Crawl, crawl
into the tunnel
As fast as you can.
But the fox caught you,
Mr. Gingerbread Man!

(Collect the gingerbread men as students crawl out.)

44

Gingerbread Man (cont.)

Directions to Students (cont.)

Play Dough Gingerbread Man

1. Today we are going to make pretend gingerbread cookies. Get a small piece of play dough about the size of a golf ball. Roll the play dough into a ball. Using the rolling pin, roll out your dough.

2. Once your dough has been rolled out, take either a circle cookie cutter or gingerbread man cookie cutter and press it into the dough.

3. Decorate the face of your cookie. Make eyes, nose, and a mouth with the pegs.

4. Take the spatula and scoop under your cookie. Hold the spatula at shoulder level with your arm straight out in front of you. Walk over to the cookie sheet and place your cookie on it.

5. Jump, holding your feet together, back to the starting point to give the next student the spatula.

Decorating Cookies

1. Take one cookie from the tray and pick up a decorating bag or squeeze bottle filled with frosting.

2. Squeeze a small amount of frosting onto your cookie to create eyes, a nose, and a mouth.

3. Place one raisin on each dot of icing to complete your gingerbread man.

Additional Activities

1. Make play dough and add ginger and spices to it for gingerbread smells.

2. Make gingerbread cookies from scratch.

3. Have the students walk around obstacles while carrying a cookie on a spatula.

4. Have students come up with other ideas for stanzas of the poem, along with motor actions.

5. Use other candies for decorating cookies such as chocolate sprinkles, red hots, or use colored frosting.

Observations for Sensory Motor Activities

Motor Planning

• Can the student follow the motor actions of the poem, or does he or she need to watch others?
If difficult, have students go slowly.

Bilateral Integration

• Can the student gallop with either foot leading, or can he or she only do it with one foot?
If difficult, emphasize hopping on either foot.

Fine Motor

• Can the student squeeze out just one dot of frosting at a time, or does a lot of frosting get squeezed out at a time?

• Can the student hold a spatula with a cookie on it at shoulder level with his or her arm straight out in front, or are two arms needed to hold up the spatula?
If difficult, emphasize blackboard activities above shoulder level.

• Can the student carry a cookie on the spatula without dropping it, or does the cookie fall off several times before it gets to the cookie sheet?
If difficult, work on chalkboard activities and hitting a ball or balloon overhead.

Gingerbread Man (cont.)

Holiday Cookies

Materials

- 1 rolling pin or 12" (30 cm) dowel for every two students
- 1 cookie sheet or baking pan with sides
- 30 small pegs
- 2 lbs. (900 g) dried beans or rice
- 2 packages Jell-O™ (8 serving size)
- 4 mixing bowls or containers
- 2 sets of measuring cups
- 3–4 cookie cutters
- 2 large spoons
- 1 beach towel
- play dough
- spatula
- water

Teacher Preparation

1. Prepare finger Jell-O a day ahead of time. Stir $2\frac{1}{2}$ cups (600 mL) boiling water into two packages of Jell-O until completely dissolved. Pour the mixture into a cookie sheet with sides. Refrigerate.
2. Place dry rice, beans, or water in a bowl or container.
3. Set up the area for play dough with rolling pins, small pegs, and cookie cutters.
4. Place beach towel flat on the floor.

Directions to Students

Cookie Dough

1. Today you are going to be holiday cookies.
2. The first thing you are going to do is roll yourself up like cookie dough. Has anyone ever made cookies before?
3. Lie down on the end of the beach towel so your head and feet are sticking out over the edges of the towel. Have your arms at your sides.
4. Let's roll you up in the towel. (Slowly roll the child in the towel, rolling two to three times until he or she is completely rolled up.)
5. Now that you are rolled up, we are going to add butter, sprinkles, chocolate chips, nuts, and raisins to the cookie dough. (Act as if you are sticking nuts, sprinkles, etc., into the cookie dough, and state what you are doing as you are doing it.)
6. Okay cookie dough, time to unroll.

Holiday Cookies *(cont.)*

Directions to Students *(cont.)*

Pouring

1. There are mixing bowls on the table filled with dried beans, rice, and water. There are also some empty mixing bowls and measuring cups.

2. Fill two measuring cups with different ingredients and then pour the ingredients into a mixing bowl.

3. After you have poured two cups, take a large spoon and mix your ingredients together. Is it easy to stir the ingredients you chose?

Roll Out Cookie Dough

1. Find a partner. One student is the cookie dough, and the other is the baker.

2. The cookie dough partner needs to lie flat on his or her stomach on the floor.

3. The baker partner needs to roll out the cookie dough, using the rolling pin (or dowel). Roll out the arms, legs, and back.

4. When finished rolling, draw a simple shape on the cookie dough student's back. Use your index finger for drawing. See if the cookie dough student can guess what shape you drew.

5. Trade places when the cookie dough student is finished guessing.

Bake the Cookies

1. Now that you have been rolled up and rolled out, you cookies (students) are ready to be baked.

2. Three cookies can be baked at a time. Stand in a row, so that all three fit on the cookie sheet (towel).

3. The three cookies need to squat down as small as they can. The class is going to count to 10. When the class says "10," the three cookies need to pop up like they are cookies that have finished baking.

4. Continue until all students have had a turn being a cookie.

Play Dough Cookies

1. Get a small piece of play dough about the size of a golfball. Roll it into a ball, using both hands.

2. Place it on the table and use a rolling pin or dowel to roll it out.

3. Pick a cookie cutter to press into the play dough.

4. Decorate your play dough cookie with pegs.

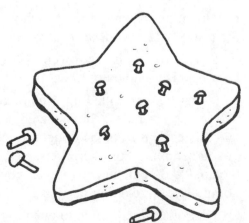

Holiday Cookies *(cont.)*

Directions to Students *(cont.)*

Finger Jell-O™ Cookies

1. On the table, we have some finger Jell-O and cookie cutters. Everyone gets to make one Jell-O cookie.
2. Pick out a cookie cutter, push it down into the Jell-O, and then pull the cookie cutter up.
3. Use your fingers or the spatula to pick up your cookie. As soon as everyone has one, we can gobble them up!

Additional Activities

1. Write an alphabet letter or a number on the student's back when rolling out the cookie dough.
2. When pouring ingredients have the student use 1 cup (240 mL), ½ cup (120 mL), and ¼ cup (60 mL) measurement containers. Ask for 1 cup (240 mL) of beans or rice. Ask how many ½ cups (120 mL) or ¼ cups (60 mL) it will take to make 1 cup (240 mL).
3. Have the student climb into a large box (oven) and pop up or crawl out when a timer goes off to signal the cookie is baked.
4. Have students make "moon balls." Mix ½ cup (120 mL) honey, 1 cup (240 mL) peanut butter, and 1½ cups (360 mL) powdered milk. Form the mixture into one-inch (2.54 cm) balls and roll the balls into 1⅓ cups (320 mL) of crushed flake cereal.

Observations for Sensory Motor Activities

Motor Planning

- Can the student keep his or her arms at his or her side when being rolled up?
- Can the student assist with rolling up in the towel, or do his or her arms come out of the towel?

If difficult, have the student practice rolling.

Body Awareness

- Can the student identify shapes or letters drawn on his or her back and reproduce the same shapes?

If difficult, just draw straight horizontal lines.

Tactile Awareness

- Can the student tolerate being rolled up in towel, or is there resistance?
- Can the student tolerate having another student draw a shape on his or her back, or does he or she say it hurts or feels itchy?

If rolling up in a towel is uncomfortable for the student, try rolling the student over just one time. Build up to completely rolling up in the towel as the student becomes more comfortable.

Fine Motor

- Can the student pour with accuracy, or do the ingredients go all over the table?

If difficult, work on erasing, drawing, and other shoulder activities at the chalkboard.

- Can students roll out play dough, use the cookie cutters, and decorate the cookies, or is the activity too difficult for him or her?

If difficult, break the activity down into smaller steps.

Holiday Toys

Materials

- 1 jack-in-the-box toy
- 1 small toy train
- 3 scooter boards
- 3' (91 cm) rope
- masking tape
- 3 dreidels or spinning toys
- play dough

Teacher Preparation

1. Gather all the above materials.
2. Tie a knot in each end of the rope.

Directions to Students

Today we are going to be holiday toys—first a train, then a jack-in-the-box, and then a dreidel.

Holiday Train

1. To make a train, we need three students to lie on their stomachs on the scooter boards. The first student is the engine. The second student is the passenger car and needs to hold the legs of the the student who is the engine. The third student is the caboose and needs to hold the legs of the the student who is the passenger car.

2. The student who is the engine will hold onto one end of the rope and another student will hold the other end of the rope, pulling the train.

3. Everyone will get a turn at pulling the train and also at being part of the train.

Note: For younger students, you may want your train to be one or two scooter boards long instead of three. The distance the train travels depends on your classroom size and the strength of your students. If scooter boards are unavailable, try a skateboard or have students stand in a line and put their hands on the waist of the person in front of them to form a train.

Jack-in-the-Box

1. Now we are going to be jack-in-the-boxes just like this one. (Demonstrate with the toy jack-in-the-box.)

2. Squat down and make yourselves as small as possible.

3. When the jack-in-the-box pops up, everyone needs to jump up. (You many need to demonstrate.) Okay, everyone squat down, (start turning handle to jack-in-the-box), and remember to pop up when the jack-in-the-box pops up.

Holiday Toys *(cont.)*

Directions to Students *(cont.)*

Dreidel

1. Does everyone know what a dreidel is? A dreidel is a spinning top that is used in a game that is played during Hanukkah. (Show the dreidel and demonstrate how it spins.)
2. Each of you is going to be a dreidel. When it is your turn, I want you to slowly turn around. As you are turning, an adult will wrap tape around your waist. (This works best when the adult is sitting on a chair.)
3. After you turn three or four times, stop, and then take the tape off.
4. After you have taken the tape off, squeeze it into a small ball and throw it in the trash.

Note: If students get dizzy, have them do push-offs against the wall or floor. This deep pressure helps calm the system and gets rid of the dizziness.

Spinning Dreidels

1. On the table are some dreidels. Take turns spinning the dreidels.
2. Hold them between your thumb, index, and middle fingers. Then quickly move your thumb forward, twisting your fingers in the opposite direction. (Demonstrate.)
3. Sing "The Dreidel Song" while playing with the dreidels.

Train Track

1. Get a small (grape-size) flattened piece of play dough.
2. Roll the play dough in your fingers and make it into a ball. Roll the play dough with your thumb, index, and middle fingers to form the ball.
3. When your name is called, put your ball next to the one on the table so a track can be formed for the train.
4. When we finish our track, we will take turns running the toy train over it. Move the train on top of the track in a gentle motion.

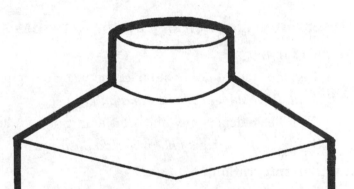

I have a little dreidel.
I made it out of clay.
And when it's dry and ready,
Oh, dreidel I shall play.

Dreidel, dreidel, dreidel,
I made it out of clay,
When it's dry and ready,
Oh, dreidel I shall play.

Holiday Toys (cont.)

Additional Activities

1. Let students take turns turning the handle of the toy jack-in-the-box. Use a cardboard box as a prop.
2. Have students squat down. When you call a name, that student gets to jump up and then squat back down.
3. Instead of using masking tape to wrap around the student being a dreidel, use a long fabric streamer. Have the student hold one end of the streamer and turn. Hold the other end of the streamer until the student is wrapped up.
4. Have students roll play dough into balls, using only the thumb, index, and middle fingers of one hand.

Observations for Sensory Motor Activities

Motor Planning

- Can the student hold onto the rope when being pulled, or does he or she let go of the rope?

If difficult, hold student's hands and pull.

- Can the student spin without difficulty, or does he or she get dizzy?

If student gets dizzy, have him or her do push-ups.

Bilateral Integration

- Can the student hold onto his or her legs in front of him or her using two hands, or is only one hand used?

If difficult, work on two-handed activities.

- Can the student take the masking tape off his or her waist by using two hands and moving his or her hands around the body, or does he or she hold onto the tape with one hand and try to spin to unwrap the tape?

If difficult, assist the student in pulling the end of the tape.

Tactile Awareness

- Can the student roll play dough using his or her fingertips, or are palms used?
- Can the student hold onto another student's feet when being a train, or are hands withdrawn?

If difficult, let the student rub his or her hands on the carpet for deep pressure prior to the activity.

Body Awareness

- Can the student spin a dreidel by moving thumb and fingers, or does he or she need to use whole arm movements?

If difficult, have student lie on his or her stomach with forearms on the ground.

Fine Motor

- Can the student roll play dough into a ball, or does it look like a worm?

If difficult, encourage more back and forth hand motions like hand washing.

Stars and Sparkle

Materials

- 2 empty plastic water bottles per student
- container (dishpan or shoebox)
- roll of clear packing tape
- glow-in-the-dark stars
- yellow construction paper
- blown-up yellow balloon
- star pattern (page 56)
- roll of two-sided tape
- 2 pounds (.9 kg) rice
- classroom table
- two-handed bat
- flashlight
- play dough
- scissors
- blanket

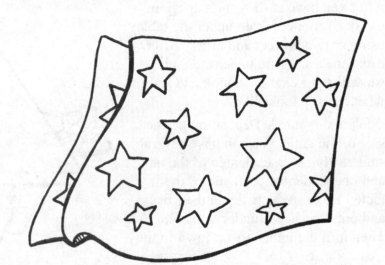

Teacher Planning

1. Cut the bottoms off the plastic water bottles. With half of these bottles, cut six slits about 2" (5 cm) up from the bottom. Space the six slits fairly evenly. Push the plastic bottle with the slits inside the other bottle until they are snug. Tape where the bottles join, using clear packing tape. This is a two-handed bat.

2. Cut several stars out of yellow construction paper, using the pattern. These can be laminated. Make at least 10 large stars and eight small stars.

3. Place dried rice into a container such as a plastic dishpan or a shoebox. Later, glow-in-the-dark stars will be hidden in this container.

4. Have two-sided tape available to put on the back of the yellow construction paper stars.

5. Place the blanket over a table.

6. Place glow-in-the-dark stars and play dough at one end of a table.

Directions to Students

Stars in the Sky

1. Who has looked up into the sky at night and seen stars? Does anyone know what a star is? Stars look like points of light in the night sky. Today we are going to put our own stars in the sky. You will take a small piece of play dough about the size of a grape, and roll it in your fingers until it is a ball. Then pick out one glow-in-the-dark star, and put the ball of play dough on the back of it.

2. Lie on your back and scoot under the table using just your feet and elbows. When you get under the table, reach up and push your star on the bottom of the table. The play dough will make it stick.

Stars and Sparkle *(cont.)*

Directions to Students *(cont.)*

Stars in the Sky *(cont.)*

3. After you have stuck your star up in the sky, scoot out from under the table, using only your feet and arms. After everyone's stars are under the table, we will get a chance to look and see what our sky looks like.

4. Look at our stars! (Depending on the size of the table, you can have several students lying on each side of the table and one student at each end of the table. Have students lie on their backs and put their heads under the table. Then turn the lights off or down in the classroom.)

Falling Stars

1. Here are some two-handed bats and a blown-up yellow balloon. Lay on your stomachs in a circle with your heads pointing towards the center. Have about one arm's length between each of you.

2. You are now going to hit our falling star. Does anyone know what a falling star is? A falling star looks like a bright streak of light in the sky.

3. Each of you will receive a two-handed bat. Do you know why it is called a two-handed bat? It is because you always use two hands when holding it.

4. The balloon will be dropped into the circle. It will be our falling star. When the balloon comes to you, hit it so it stays in the air. How long can we keep the falling star up in the air before it falls? Remember, use two hands.

5. Let's count how long you can hit the falling star (balloon) before it touches the ground.

6. That was fun. Please pick up all the two-handed bats and the balloon, and we will put them away.

Star in the Sky

1. Let's sit on the floor. Here is a flashlight. When we turn it on, it will be pointed to the ceiling. We will turn off the lights. Is everyone ready for the lights to go off?

2. Does everyone see my star? Follow the star with your index finger.

3. Follow the star with your pointer finger. (Go fast, go slow. Go on the ceiling and then the walls, the floor, and on your shoes.)

Note: If you turn the lights down in your room, it is easier for students to see the light. A laser pointer works best, but many school districts no longer allow its use.

Stars and Sparkle *(cont.)*

Directions to Students *(cont.)*

Search for the Stars

1. There are several glow-in-the-dark stars hidden in the container of dried rice.

2. Can each of you find two stars? Find one star with your right hand and find one star with your left hand.

3. After you have pulled two stars out of the rice, hide them in the rice again for the next student to find.

Jumping Star to Star

1. Do you see the yellow paper stars on the floor?

2. You are going to jump from star to star. When your name is called, stand up and jump with both feet from star to star.

3. Let's try to hop this time. What else can we try? How about walking backwards, or walking on tiptoes, or on heels? How about putting your hands on the stars, instead of your feet?

Stars on Students

1. Each of you will have stars placed on you, attached with two-sided tape. At least two stars will be placed on the front of you and two stars on your back.

2. Try not to look while you feel for the stars and then take them off.

3. Return the stars so they can be placed on the next student.

Additional Activities

1. Have students determine if the stars they are picking up are small-, medium-, or large-sized.

2. Sing "Twinkle, Twinkle Little Star" while students are lying under the table viewing the stars. Have students count the stars.

3. Tape a large piece of paper underneath the tabletop. Have students lie on their backs under the table and draw stars on the paper.

4. Have students lift their elbows off the floor when using the two-handed bat. This will develop shoulder strength.

5. Add sand, rice, or beans to the two-handed bats to make them heavier. Add bells, beads, or glitter stars to the inside of the two-handed bats for added interest.

6. Put numbers on paper stars and have students jump in numerical order.

Stars and Sparkle (cont.)

Additional Activities (cont.)

7. Write a letter on each star. Give students a word and have them jump to the letters that will spell the word out.

8. Write students' names on the paper stars. Call out a name and have students take turns jumping to the name that is called out.

9. Have students close their eyes when finding stars in the rice.

10. Instead of paper stars, have students remove star stickers from their clothing.

Observations for Sensory Motor Activities

Motor Planning

- Can the student scoot under the table using just elbows and feet, or does he or she roll over on one side or stomach to scoot?
- Can the student remain on his or her stomach and hit the balloon with a two-handed bat, or does he or she roll on one side and use just one hand?
- Can the student jump with two feet together and remain balanced while jumping from star to star?

If difficult, slow down the pace. Emphasize more activities done lying on the stomach.

Bilateral Integration

- Can the student use a two-handed bat, or is the balloon hit with just one hand?
- Can the student find stars in the rice and hold one star in each hand, or is the task completed one hand at a time?

If difficult, work on two-handed activities.

Body Awareness

- Can the student find stars that are placed on his or her body. Can he or she feel the stars, or does he or she need to look?

If difficult, tap the location of the stars with your finger for the student

Crossing Midline

- Can the student cross the midline with his or her finger when pointing to a star in the sky (flashlight), or does his or her whole body move?

If difficult, have the student lie on his or her stomach and place his or her forearms on the ground.

Fine Motor

- Can the student roll play dough into a ball?
- Can the student isolate his or her index finger for pointing, or does the student use his or her whole hand?

If difficult, do pegboard activities and fingerplays.

Snow Play

Materials

- 5–6 pieces of recycled paper per student
- red, blue, and yellow construction paper
- water and towels for cleanup
- 5–6' (1.5–1.8 m) clothesline
- 1 blanket or beach towel
- winged clothespins (page 8)
- mitten pattern (page 57)
- scissors
- carpet squares
- shaving cream
- chalk
- lacing thread (optional)
- hole punch (optional)
- crayons (optional)

Teacher Preparation

1. Cut out one mitten per student, using the pattern.
2. Attach the clothesline between the tops of two chairs. Have winged clothespins on the floor under the clothesline.
3. Lay the blanket or beach towel on the floor.
4. Place the can of shaving cream on the table.
5. Place the carpet squares and chalk on the floor.
6. Have water and towels for clean-up nearby.

Directions to Students

Sled

1. Today we are going to pretend we are playing in the snow.
2. This is our sled (blanket or beach towel). One student is going to sit or lie on the "sled" and get taken for a ride.
3. Have two students stand at one end and hold the corners of the blanket.
4. The rider needs to hold on tight while the two students pull the sled (blanket or beach towel).

Note: Depending on how strong your students are, you can have them follow a trail or just pull the sled up to a certain point and then back to the beginning.

Snowball

1. Get five or six pieces of paper or newspaper.
2. Now you are going to make a snowball. Take one piece of paper and squeeze it real tight to make a snowball.
3. Take your next piece of paper, put it over your snowball, and squeeze it.
4. Watch your snowball get bigger! Continue adding paper until all your paper is gone.
5. Who has the smallest snowball? Who has the largest?
6. Our snowballs are melting. Take off one piece of paper at a time until your snowball is gone.

Snow Play *(cont.)*

Directions to Students *(cont.)*

Mittens

1. Now that we have played in the snow our mittens and hands are all wet, we need to hang our mittens up to dry. Does everyone have one or two paper mittens?
2. Take turns coming up to our clothesline, picking up the winged clothespins, and hanging your mitten to dry.

Snow Angels

1. How many of you have ever played in the snow? How many of you have ever made angels in the snow or in the sand?
2. You are going to make angels in the snow today. Lie down on your backs on the floor. Spread out. You are going to move your arms and legs, and you don't want to bump into your neighbor.
3. Move your arms and legs out away from your body and then bring them into your body. Watch me. We are going to do this together slowly.
4. Make sure your arms go above your head and that both arms and legs move together at the same time.

Designs in Snow

1. Everyone gets to take his or her shoes and socks off. Place your socks inside your shoes so they don't get mixed up.
2. Draw a simple design on the carpet square using the chalk. Imagine you are drawing in the snow.
3. After you finish your design, erase it by using your feet. Use both feet to erase. Stand up and erase it well so the chalk design is gone.
4. If you have time, draw a second design and erase it with your hands.

Shaving Cream Art

1. Let's put shaving cream down on our table. Doesn't it look like snow?
2. Make a design in the shaving cream with your fingers. Make shapes, or write names, the alphabet, or spelling words.
3. With a partner, draw a picture in the shaving cream.
4. Wash and dry your hands after you finish.

Additional Activities

1. Have students pull the sled around different obstacles.
2. Have just one student pulling the sled by grasping both corners of the blanket.
3. Have the student roll, crawl, hop, or walk backwards to the sled.
4. Have one student squeeze one paper into a small snowball and pass it to the next student to add the next paper to make the snowball bigger. Reverse the process.
5. Throw snowballs at a target. A good target is the trash can to finish the activity.
6. Have students cut out their own mittens.
7. Have each student make a right and a left mitten. Have students cut out their own mittens and decorate them so they match. Have students punch holes along the outer edge and lace the mittens together.

58

Snow Play (cont.)

Observations for Sensory Motor Activities

Motor Planning

- Can the student hold onto the sled and pull it with an adequate amount of strength without falling down?

- Can the student hold the sled with one or two hands and pull, or does he or she let go of the blanket?

- Can the student maintain balance when sitting on the sled as it is being pulled, or does he or she fall off?

If difficult, slow down the pace until students are successful.

- Can the student move his or her arms and legs simultaneously to make angels in the snow?

If difficult, have the student slow down. Have the student hold the beanbags in his or her hands to draw attention to what their hands are doing.

Bilateral Integration

- Can the student hold onto the mitten with one hand and the clothespin with the other hand and hang the mitten, or are two hands needed on the winged clothespin?

- Can the student squeeze the snowball tightly, or is the snowball loose and falling apart?

If difficult, practice two-handed activities.

- Can the student draw circles or lines using both hands in the shaving cream at the same time, or can he or she only use one hand at a time?

If difficult, draw on the chalkboard with two hands simultaneously.

Fine Motor

- Can the student hang the mittens up, or is the student unable to use the clothespins?

- Can the student color the mittens so they match?

If difficult, guide students through the activity. Practice picking up items with tongs and using play dough.

Tactile Awareness

- Can the student hold onto the chalk, or does the texture feel funny and cause the student to refuse to hold it?

- Can the student wipe the chalk design off using his or her feet, or does he or she withdraw?

- Can the student put whole hands in shaving cream, or only one fingertip at a time?

- Can the student work in shaving cream, or does he or she immediately want to go wash his or her hands?

If difficult, have student rub his or her hands together briskly on the carpet before the activity starts. Encourage play in textures such as beans or rice.

Snow

Materials

- several sheets of newspapers per student
- flat, twin-sized bedsheet
- one hand towel or washcloth per student
- 2–3 pages of tissue paper or pages from an old phone book
- quarter
- ice tongs—one per group of four students
- large plastic mixing bowl or plastic container

Teacher Preparation

Other than gathering materials, no advance preparation is needed.

Directions to Students

Snowballs

1. Has anyone lived in a place where it snows or gone to the mountains in the wintertime? If you have, you've probably packed snow to make a snowball. You have to pack the snow into a tight little ball so that it stays together. Today we're going to make "pretend snowballs" out of newspaper and build a mountain with our snowballs.

2. Everyone join hands and form a circle. Drop your hands and take three steps backwards. The sheet will be spread in the middle and each of you will receive some newspaper.

3. We'll tear a full sheet of newspaper in half. Place both hands on the top edge of the newspaper. Keep your left hand still while you pull the newspaper toward your body with your right hand. Left-handers may want to keep their right hand still while pulling newspaper toward their bodies with their left hand. Once the paper is torn, begin to crumble it.

4. To get our snowballs to be as small as possible, squeeze the paper as hard as you can as you crumble your newspaper into a "snowball."

5. Throw your snowball onto the sheet when you finish it and it is as tight as you can make it. To build a mountain, we'll need to make lots more newspaper snowballs!

6. It's time to play in the snow! Who can walk over the snowball mountain? crawl under the mountain of snowballs? crawl backward over the mountain? roll over the mountain? stand on this wooden block and jump into the pile of snowballs?

7. We've had a fun time playing in the snow. Now, it's time to dry ourselves off with these towels so we don't get chilled. Hold your hand towel in your right hand and rub your left arm until it's dry. Remember to dry your shoulder, elbow, wrist, and fingers! Let's dry our left legs. Start with the thigh, then dry the knee, ankle, and, last of all, foot. Time to switch the towel to the left hand. Dry your right arm and leg. Choose a partner and dry each other's backs.

Snow *(cont.)*

Directions to Students *(cont.)*

Snowflakes

1. Sometimes when it snows, the snowflakes are as big as this quarter. At other times, the snowflakes are smaller than your little fingernail. Today we're going to tear paper to make snowflakes.
2. Each of you will receive one sheet of paper from the telephone book. Tear it into snowflakes about the size of this quarter. How many quarter-sized snowflakes do you think you can tear from one page?
3. Pretend that the snowflakes are so cold that they would sting our fingers if we touched them. Let's pick them up using these ice tongs and drop them in this bowl.

Additional Activities

1. Make snowballs and snowflakes out of different weights of paper, e.g., construction paper, wax paper, copy paper. The heavier the paper, the stronger the hands have to be.
2. Graph the student's estimates of the number of snowflakes they will tear from one telephone page, and an actual number they tore that are as large as a quarter.
3. Clean up the snowflakes from the floor by crumpling them into little balls, and pushing them into the narrow opening of a plastic soda bottle.

Observations for Sensory Motor Activities

Motor Planning

- Did the student hesitate and need time to think about how to crawl backwards?
- Can the student keep his or her tummy on the floor while crawling?

If not, provide gentle downward pressure on his or her back so that he or she gets the sensation of crawling with the tummy in contact with the floor.

Body Awareness

- Notice whether the student located and "dried" body parts named, or whether he or she waited for the teacher or other students to demonstrate where to dry.

Slow pace if student was struggling to follow directions.

Bilateral Integration

- When drying off after playing in the snow, did the student easily rub his or her opposite leg and arm with the towel?

If not, refer to the Bilateral Integration section at the opening of this book for suggestions to help students develop the ability to cross arms and legs over midline.

Tactile Awareness

- Did the student verbalize discomfort when rubbing his or her arms and legs with a towel?

If student resists specific tactile sensations, he or she may tolerate these sensations better while moving. Try having him or her sit on a playground ball as he or she "dries" arms and legs.

Fine Motor

- Could the student operate the tongs to pick up paper scraps off the floor?

Some tongs are easier to operate than others. Begin with tongs that have a gentle spring action and work up to tongs that are stiffer to operate. Also, it's easier to operate tongs when fingers are closer to the tong ends.

Valentine Hearts

Materials

- cardboard or plastic storage box, approximately 12" x 12" x 4" deep (30 cm x 30 cm x 10 cm)
- one 8½" x 11" (22 cm x 28 cm) sheet of red, white, or pink construction paper per student
- 1 cardboard heart pattern per student
- scraps of ribbon, wallpaper, doilies
- 18 hula hoops or plastic rings
- 10–12' (3 m–3.6 m) clothesline
- 2 craft sticks per student
- 4 clothespins per student
- 4 envelopes per student
- 4 stickers per student
- 1 scissors per student
- 1 pencil per student
- small handsaw
- masking tape
- 18 beanbags
- white glue, paste
- sandpaper

Teacher Preparation

1. Arrange the hula hoops on the floor in a heart pattern. Tape the hoops down on either side to hold them loosely in place.
2. Attach a clothesline between two chairs so it is about three to four feet (91–122 cm) off the ground.
3. Make winged clothespins. (See page 8.)
4. Set out construction paper, stickers, heart patterns, pencils, and scissors on worktables.
5. Make heart patterns for each student, using cardboard or empty cereal boxes.

Teacher Directions to Students

Hula Hoop Heart

1. Usually when we jump into hula hoops, we arrange the hoops in a straight line or a circle. However, since Valentine's Day is this month, it might be fun to arrange the hoops in a heart pattern. Who thinks they can go around the heart while jumping one time in each hoop?
2. You did so well jumping around the heart, let's try something a little more challenging! I need a helper to drop one beanbag inside each hoop and another helper to put this box in the middle of the hula hoop heart.
3. Now we're ready to jump into a hoop, squat down and pick up a beanbag, and toss the beanbag into the box.

Valentine Hearts *(cont.)*

Directions to Students *(cont.)*

Making Valentines and Hanging Them Out to Dry

1. Taking time to do something nice or to make something pretty for someone is a great way to show that you care for them. Today we're going to make and decorate our own valentines.

2. First, you'll need to place the heart pattern on your paper. Be sure that you can see construction paper all around the edges of the pattern.

3. Hold the pattern down securely with one hand while you trace around the edges.

4. Carefully cut out the heart you traced. Use the paper scraps, pieces of ribbon, stickers, etc., to decorate the heart.

5. When you're finished making your valentines, we're going to hang them up to dry. Before we had clothes dryers, everyone used to wash their clothes and hang them up on a clothesline until they were dry.

6. Today we're going to hang up our valentines until the glue/paste dries. We're going to use some special clothespins that help your hands get strong. These clothespins have half of a craft stick glued on one handle. Your thumb holds onto the clothespin handle and the other four fingers all go on this craft stick. When you press the clothespin open, the muscles in your palms work really hard and this helps your hand get strong.

Getting Valentines Ready to Mail

1. Our valentines are dry. It's time to take them off the clothesline and put them into envelopes. When you take them off the clothesline, remember to put your four fingertips on the clothespin crossbar and press on the handle to release your valentine.

2. Sign your valentine and address the envelope to the person who is to receive it.

3. Fold your valentine carefully to fit it into the envelope.

Note: Some students may need help addressing valentines.

Additional Activities

1. Jump backwards along the hula hoop heart. Jump sideways along the hula hoop heart.

2. If you're studying fractions, practice folding construction paper into halves or quarters to make two or four hearts from one piece of paper.

Valentine Hearts (cont.)

Observations for Sensory Motor Activities

Motor Planning

- Does the student jump smoothly and rhythmically from one hula hoop to the next?
- Does the student clear the edges of the hoops when jumping from one into another?

If not, provide a small trampoline or foam rubber blocks to give the student the sensation of jumping up high, then return to jumping from one hoop to the next.

Body Awareness

- Can the student jump forward, backwards, and sideways, and land inside the hoops?
- Does the student get dizzy, disoriented, or wobbly when stooping over to pick up beanbags off the floor?

To alleviate dizziness, apply firm downward pressure on the student's shoulders or suggest push-ups against the wall. These heavy work activities help reduce dizziness.

Bilateral Integration and Crossing Midline

- When tracing, can the student adjust his or her handhold so that he or she can trace all around the pattern?
- Can the student hold down the heart pattern with one hand and keep it in place while tracing around pattern?

If difficult, readjust the helping hand by picking up the hand and placing it where it needs to be so that the student will get the sensation of hands working together efficiently.

Tactile

- Does the student protest the sticky feel of paste or stickers?

Work slowly towards building acceptance of textures. Initially, ask the student to put on one or two stickers and gradually increase expectations as tolerance increases. Sitting on a playground ball or a T-stool while using paste and stickers can sometimes distract the student and take the focus off the "unpleasant" tactile sensation.

Fine Motor

- Can the student position four fingertips (index, middle, ring, and little) on the craft stick crossbar of a winged clothespin?

If difficult, include more fingerplay and sign language experiences across the curriculum.

- Does the student have the strength necessary to press open the winged clothespin?
- Does the student hold the valentine against the clothesline with one hand and operate the clothespin with other hand?

If hanging items on a clothesline is too difficult, ask the student to press the clothespin open and put it on the valentine, but not on the clothesline.

- When taking a valentine off the clothesline, can student hold onto the valentine to keep it from dropping to the ground?

Guide the student's helping hand to the valentine to experience both hands working together.

Going Shopping

Materials

- obstacles (building blocks, beanbag chair, hula hoops, tiltboard, a low balance beam, table, chairs)
- 12 small rocks that will fit into the egg carton depressions
- 5 pounds (2.25 kg) of rice in a plastic storage box
- play dough, approximately ½ cup (120 mL) per student
- small round pegs, approximately 10 per student
- 1 package 3" x 5" (8 cm x 13 cm) index cards
- rolling pin, one per group of five students
- plastic measuring cups in various sizes
- 1 plastic table knife per student
- 5 empty plastic film canisters
- egg cartons and milk cartons
- 1-pound (450 g) bag of beans
- cans of vegetables or fruit
- bags of flour and sugar
- 2 large mixing bowls
- wide felt tip marker
- walnut in the shell
- roll of pennies
- 3 wooden spoons
- masking tape
- craft sticks
- backpack

Teacher Preparation

1. Weight the egg carton by placing a small rock in each depression. Wrap the egg carton with masking tape to hold it closed.

2. Weight milk carton with 1 pound (450 g) of beans and tape the top shut.

3. Set up a grocery store and arrange grocery items on the floor in this area.

4. Write appropriate money amounts for students on index cards.

5. Set up an obstacle course from the grocery store to home. Try large building blocks to go around, beanbag chairs to walk over, tables for bridges to crawl under, balance beam to walk on, and hula hoops to jump into.

6. Place 10 pennies in each film canister and put on the lids.

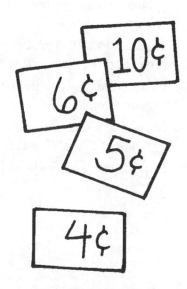

Going Shopping *(cont.)*

Directions to Students

Grocery Shopping

1. Today you're going to go grocery shopping without a list. When it's your turn, two items will be called out for you to get at the store.

2. To get to the grocery store, you'll need to go through this obstacle course. (Explain the path in the order you've arranged the equipment.)

3. Find your groceries and go to the cashier.

4. Now it's time to pay for the groceries. Let's choose a cashier. The cashier will pick an index card from the stack. There is a money amount written on each card. The shopper will pay the amount written on the card.

5. Take off the lid of the film container filled with pennies. Carefully count out the pennies and give the cashier the correct amount.

Carrying Groceries Home

1. It's a long way home! Here's a backpack to help you get the groceries back there. Unzip it, and put the groceries inside.

2. Go back through the obstacle course to get home. Be careful your backpack doesn't bump into things.

3. When you arrive home, unzip the backpack, take out the groceries, and put them on the table.

4. Reopen the cannister and count out your change.

Additional Activities

1. Prepare shopping lists as part of a writing lesson.

2. Take a trip to the grocery store to study how food is organized within the store.

3. Categorize grocery items or pictures of grocery items.

4. Introduce and reinforce money concepts when purchasing grocery items in the classroom store; e.g., substitute a nickel for five pennies or a dime for two nickels.

5. Experiment and find out how many cups of beans are needed to fill a pint, a quart, and a gallon.

Going Shopping (cont.)

Observations for Sensory Motor Activities

Motor Planning

- Can the student step over obstacles without tripping?

If not, start with smaller items to step over and gradually increase the size as students are able.

- Does the student remember wearing the backpack and lower his or her body enough so that the backpack doesn't hang up on the table "bridge"?
- Can the student go through obstacle path in reversed order?

If difficult, start with fewer obstacles and provide pictures in the sequence they need to follow.

- Can the student put on the backpack without adult assistance?
- Can the student adjust his or her balance to walk on a variety of obstacles when the loaded backpack is on his or her shoulders?

If the weight shifts too freely within the pack, tighten the backpack straps or use an additional piece of cloth to tie the backpack to the child's trunk.

Bilateral Coordination

- Can the student hold the backpack open with one hand while using the other hand to put items into and take items out of the backpack?

Guide the student's helping hand into place on the backpack, if necessary.

Tactile Awareness

- Does student resist working with play dough?

Some students tolerate tactile experiences better if they are moving while working with play dough. Have student try squeezing and shaping play dough while sitting on a rocker balance board or in a rocker boat.

Fine Motor Experiences

- Is student able to open the lid of the plastic film canister and replace the cap securely?

If the lid is too small, use margarine tubs, as their lids are often easier than film canister lids to remove and replace.

Playing Letter Carrier

Materials

- various-sized boxes, including one larger sturdy box to be used as a delivery truck
- stepping stones or foam rubber squares, approximately 6" (15 cm) on a side
- package of 4" x 6" (10 cm x 15 cm) index cards
- 3–4 business-sized envelopes per student
- 1 adhesive address label per student
- 3–4 address labels per student
- several stickers per student
- ink pad and rubber stamps
- 4' (1.2 m) rope
- 6–7 carpet squares
- old telephone book
- masking tape
- marking pen
- 2 bricks
- scissors
- backpack

Teacher Preparation

1. Prepare the sturdy box to be used as a delivery truck. Using scissors, carefully poke a hole in the middle of one side of the sturdy box. Form a rope handle by pushing both ends of the rope through the hole and knotting both ends together on the inside of the box. Weight the "truck" by placing one or two bricks inside the box.

2. Make an obstacle path for the truck, using classroom furniture. To form a road for the truck, arrange chairs in two rows with approximately 3' (1 m) between the rows. Arrange worktables to form bridges under which to travel. Waste baskets or desks can be placed in the obstacle course to represent trees or buildings.

3. Designate places in the room to be delivery sites.

4. Make a walking path for the letter carrier. Place carpet squares on the floor to represent puddles. Arrange stepping stones or foam rubber squares on the floor to represent the walking path.

5. Using a marking pen, write a house numeral and street name on each envelope. Write corresponding numerals and street names on large index cards and tape the cards on chairs or tables that will serve as houses.

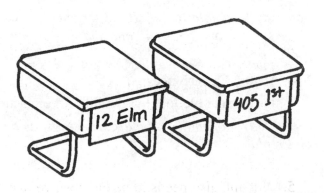

6. Print or type each student's address on a separate adhesive label.

68

Playing Letter Carrier *(cont.)*

Directions to Students

Delivering Packages

1. People who deliver packages to homes and businesses have to be good, safe drivers. We're going to practice our driving skills today. This box with the rope handle will be our delivery truck.

2. Load the packages to be delivered into the delivery truck and pull it down the road between the row of chairs. Do you think you'll be able to drive without knocking the truck against the chairs?

3. This table will be our bridge. Get down on your hands and knees and pull the truck under the bridge.

4. You did so well delivering one package, let's see if you can deliver two packages. To get from the post office to the homes, you'll need to pull your truck between the chairs, under the bridge, and around the desk and other obstacles.

5. Deliver one box to . . . (designate area) and then deliver a box to . . . (designate second area).

Delivering Letters

1. Letter carriers have to check the envelopes very carefully to be sure that they deliver the letters to the correct house. Have you ever had mail delivered to your house that belonged to someone else? Today we're going to see how well you match the address on the envelope to the address on the "house."

2. Let's pretend it's a rainy day and there are puddles along the letter carrier's route. These carpet squares are the puddles. You'll need to jump over the puddles to get to the houses.

3. Look at the address on the first house. Find the letter that has the same number and deliver that letter. Go to the second house and find the letter that belongs there and deliver it.

Getting Letters Ready to Mail

1. After you've written a letter, you need to fold the paper so that it fits into the envelope. It takes a lot of practice to do this neatly.

2. To fold your paper, move the bottom corners up to touch the top corners. Hold the top edges in place with one hand while you press the fold flat with the other hand.

3. Fold your paper in half again; be sure the corners touch. Hold the top edges in place with one hand and press the fold with your other hand.

4. The letter carrier won't know where to deliver your letter unless you neatly print the address. Here are some address labels with your family's name and address. Remove the label from the backing and put the label in the center of the envelope.

5. A stamp also needs to be on the envelope. Here are some stickers that we can pretend are stamps. The stamp goes in the top right-hand corner.

Playing Letter Carrier (cont.)

Additional Activities

1. Work on sequencing skills (e.g., instruct students to deliver the red box to the library center, the blue box to the science center, and the green box to the music center).

2. Practice positional concepts by asking students to deliver letters under, over, beside, etc., various objects in the classroom.

3. Reinforce or teach the letters associated with letters (Ll), mail (Mm), and packages (Pp).

4. If students are learning to recognize each other's names, write the student's names on the houses and match the name on the envelope to the name on house.

5. If students are able to copy from a model, ask them to copy their addresses onto envelopes and hand deliver school notes to their parents.

Observations for Sensory Motor Activities

Motor Planning

* Is the student able to pull the delivery truck down a path without bumping it against classroom furniture?

If difficult, start with chairs further apart and gradually move them closer together as the student becomes more adept at moving. If the student bumps against an object while trying to go around it, put a masking tape line on the floor about 2 feet (61 cm) away from the object. The line is sometimes easier to follow and gives an idea of how far he or she needs to be from the object.

* Does the student remember the sequence of the delivery path?

Start with two delivery sites and add more only as the students become successful.

Body Awareness

* Does the student duck his or her head to avoid hitting the table when crawling under it?

Usually it takes just one collision to make the student more aware of where his or her head is. If this is a repeated problem, pad the edges of the table with foam rubber to prevent injury.

Bilateral Integration

* Does the student weight down paper with the helping hand while creasing paper with other hand?

If not, guide the helping hand to a position where it holds down the paper securely.

Fine Motor

* Can the student match corners when folding paper?
* Does the student leave spaces between words and between rows of words when addressing envelopes?

If the student doesn't have a good sense of spacing, write one line of the address on a tagboard strip, exaggerating the spaces between words and numerals. Ask student to cut apart address between words. (See example.)

1009	Blackwood	Street

70

Baby Animals—Bunnies

Materials

- 3 yds (2.7 m) of 48" (1.2 m) stretchy polyester (best if you can see light and shadows through the fabric when it is held up to the light)
- small plastic pitcher or plastic measuring cup with pouring spout
- enough small 2½" (6 cm) balls to fill two copier paper boxes (balls similar to those found in ball rooms)
- adult medium size elasticized gym shorts, one per group of five
- children's jacket or weighted vest, one per group of five
- 4 plastic cups from children's toy dish sets
- 1 parboiled carrot strip per student
- 4' (1.2 m) clothesline or rope
- children's plastic teapot
- 5 carpet squares
- small parachute
- spool of thread
- stuffed bunny
- large pitcher
- water

Teacher Preparation

1. Sew a drawstring bag for the plastic bubble balls, using the stretchy fabric. Fold the stretchy polyester fabric in half so that the selvaged edges match on the sides. Sew the sides and bottom ¾" (2 cm) from edges. Make a casing on the top raw edge by folding the top edge down 2" (5 cm) and stitching the flap ¼" (.6 cm) from the raw edge, leaving 2" (5 cm) of the raw edge unsewn. Feed the rope through the opening and securely tie the rope ends together. Fill the bag about half full with plastic balls.

2. Fill a large pitcher with water to be used to fill students' smaller pitchers. Set out cups and pitchers (measuring cups) on a table.

3. Set up pathways for bunnies to follow to get to Mr. McGregor's farm, e.g., chairs to go around, carpet squares to hop over, tables to crawl under. Set out jackets and shorts at the beginning of the path.

Directions to Students

Pouring Tea for Peter Rabbit

1. Peter Rabbit was very thirsty after running away from Mr. McGregor, and he wanted a cup of tea. Each of you will get a turn to pour a cup of tea for Peter Rabbit.

2. We'll use these small pitchers and play cups. Try to pour carefully so that you don't spill any tea.

3. Take turns pouring tea for each other.

Baby Animals—Bunnies *(cont.)*

Directions to Students *(cont.)*

Bunny Hop to Bunny Hollow

1. Bunnies like to make their homes underground. They dig tunnels to get to larger underground spaces where they sleep, keep dry in stormy weather, and escape from their predators. Today we're going to pretend that we're bunnies and hop to our bunny home.

2. To hop like a bunny we need to squat down and put our palms flat on the floor. First move your hands forward, keeping your hands flat on the floor. Hop your feet forward closer to your hands.

3. Keep hopping until you get to the bag filled with small plastic balls. This bag is our pretend bunny hole. Crawl into the bunny hole and wiggle around in the balls until you get to the bottom of the "tunnel." If you'd like, you can keep your head outside of the bag.

Jumping Bunnies

1. Bunnies are really good at jumping. If we all work together, we can get this stuffed bunny to hop!

2. First, join hands and form a circle.

3. The parachute is in the center of our circle and the bunny is in the center of the parachute. Take hold of one loop with both of your hands.

4. To make the bunny jump up in the air, we have to bring our arms up at the same time and then quickly bring our arms down. Are you ready? Arms up! Arms down!

Dress Like Peter Rabbit

1. A woman named Beatrix Potter wrote a story about a bunny called Peter Rabbit. That bunny dressed up in pants and a jacket and shoes before going out to play. His mother told him to stay away from Mr. McGregor's farm, but the vegetables were ripe and Peter Rabbit loved the vegetables in that garden. Today we're going to dress up like Peter Rabbit and pretend that we're hopping to Mr. McGregor's garden.

2. I will divide you into groups. Each group will form a line. When you hear the word GO, the first student in each line will put on the shorts and the jacket. As soon as you're dressed, you'll hop to Mr. McGregor's garden.

3. First, you'll hop around the chairs, then jump over the carpet squares, and, last, crawl under the table. There will be several bunnies hopping at the same time, so be careful not to bump into other bunnies.

4. When you finish going through the obstacle course, jump back along the side to get back to your line.

5. Take off the shorts and the jacket and hand them to the next student in line. Continue until everyone has had a turn.

Baby Animals—Bunnies *(cont.)*

Directions to Students *(cont.)*

Carrots for Supper

1. Bunnies love to eat carrots! Here are some parboiled carrots for you to try today.
2. Try to bite off a piece of carrot with your molars instead of your front teeth.
3. When you're finished chewing, try biting off a second piece using your front teeth. Which is easier?

Additional Activities

1. Read Beatrix Potter's *Peter Rabbit,* and then act out the story with props and/or puppets.
2. As pouring accuracy improves, introduce slightly larger pitchers or slightly smaller cups.
3. After biting and chewing carrots, study different teeth, where they're located in the mouth, and their functions.
4. Plant carrot seeds and watch them grow. Find out what happens if some seeds are deprived of sun and/or water.

Observations for Sensory Motor Activities

Motor Planning

- Does the student coordinate the bunny jump, moving hands first and then feet?
- Can the student figure out how to hold the bag open while getting into the balls?
- Can the student get into the large shorts without help?

If difficult, place his or her hands on the waistband, holding your hands on top. When the student's foot is partially in the pants leg, remove your hands to give him or her a chance to finish without your help.

Body Awareness

- Does the student go around, under, and over obstacles without bumping into them?
- Can the student place a carrot strip on his or her molars?

Student may need a mirror so that he or she can see his or herself while doing the activity.

Bilateral Integration and Crossing Midline

- Is the student able to pour from one container to another without spilling?

If not, provide lots of pouring practice in the sand pile to develop this skill.

Baby Animals—Ducklings

Materials

- 12" x 18" (30 cm x 46 cm) brown construction paper, laminated
- 10 small plastic ducks (similar to plastic counting bears)
- one medium to large plastic rectangular storage bin
- lid to copier-paper box or similar-sized box lid
- bag of miniature marshmallows
- roll of waxed paper
- 4 slotted spoons
- 10 beanbags
- scissors
- water

Teacher Preparation

1. Tear waxed paper into 5" x 6" (13 cm x 15 cm) pieces, and then cut these strips in half. Each student will need one piece.

2. Fill the plastic rectangular storage bin half-full with water and float the plastic ducks.

3. Arrange an obstacle course for the duck parade. Arrange two rows of chairs about 3' (.9 m) apart. Clear the area around one table or desk for the students to walk around.

Directions to Students

Duckling Parade

1. Soon after baby ducklings hatch out of their shells, the mother duck leads them to water for swimming lessons. Those baby ducklings instinctively know how to walk in line, one behind the other! Let's pretend that we're ducklings who are headed to the lake for our first swim.

2. Help me choose someone to be the mother duck. Everyone line up behind the mother duck. Be sure to leave some space between you and the duckling in front of you.

3. Now, squat down and place your hands around your ankles. Stay squatting down while you walk. Try to stay in line as you walk (waddle).

4. It's a long way to the river. There are lots of obstacles along the way. Let's pretend that this table is a large building and these chairs are trees. To get to the river, we'll need to walk around the building and between this row of trees.

Baby Animals—Ducklings *(cont.)*

Directions to Students *(cont.)*

Diving for Food

1. A duck's favorite foods are the plants that grow in ponds and lakes. They swim along and pretty soon you'll see their feet up in the air! They've dipped their heads under water and they're nibbling on the plants growing on the lake bottom.

2. Today we're going to eat like the ducks do—without hands, or spoons, or forks! Let's all kneel on the ground and then sit back on our heels. Fold your "wings" behind you like this (demonstrate clasping hands behind your back.)

3. I'll put a piece of waxed paper in front of each of you and some marshmallows on the paper. Bend over and get one marshmallow at a time in your "beak." Can you get your marshmallows without falling over?

Scooping Up Ducks

1. Our plastic ducks are floating in this imaginary pond. The sides of the container are so high that the ducklings need help getting out of the water. We're going to use this slotted spoon to scoop out one duck at a time. Put it on the brown laminated paper, and scoop again until you've taken four ducks out of the water.

2. You did so well scooping up one duck at a time. Do you think you can scoop up two ducks at a time?

Teaching Ducks a New Trick

1. Ducks use their webbed feet for walking and for paddling in the water. Let's see if we can show them how to use their feet to pick up beanbags.

2. Sit on the floor in a circle. There is a box lid in the center of our circle and a beanbag in front of each of you.

3. Lean back on your hands and pick up a beanbag between your feet. Can you lift your feet up off the ground and drop the beanbag into the box?

Additional Activities

1. Teach the song, "Little White Duck", and sing this song while students are on their way to the "water" to dive for food.

Little White Duck

There's a little white duck
Sittin' in the water.
A little white duck
Doing what he ought-er.

He took a bite of a lily pad,
Flapped his wings and he said, "I'm glad
I'm a little white duck
Sittin' in the water."
Quack! Quack! Quack!

2. Read Robert McCloskey's *Make Way for Ducklings*. Ask students if they have ever seen a mother duck leading her ducklings to water. Did they stay in a straight line? Were they good divers?

3. Plan a trip to a local park, farm, or zoo to see baby ducklings.

Baby Animals—Ducklings (cont.)

Observations for Sensory Motor Activities

Motor Planning

- Can the student hold onto his or her ankles and walk forward while in a squatting position?

If balance is poor, student may need to put his or her hands on knees while walking, or have an adult hold his or her shoulders for stability.

- Can the student remain kneeling and maintain balance while "diving" for marshmallows?
- Can the student hold a beanbag securely between his or her two feet while transporting the beanbag to the box?

Use feet to pick up objects while sitting or lying on the floor. It is a great way to develop abdominal muscles for good sitting posture. Give many opportunities to practice this activity.

Body Awareness

- Does the student focus on the box when dropping the beanbag, or does he or she watch his or her feet the whole time the beanbag is being transported?

If difficult, have the student lift his or her feet up off the floor. Position feet about 12" (30 cm) above the box lid. Place the beanbag between the student's feet, and have him or her hold the beanbag for a count of five before dropping it into the box.

- Is the student able to walk between the rows of chairs without bumping into them?

It may be necessary to leave a larger space between rows of chairs and gradually bring them closer together as student develops more control of his or her body movements.

- Can the student keep his or her hands behind his or her back when "diving" for marshmallows?

Some students dive for marshmallows without using their hands to help them balance if they are already holding something in their hands like a beanbag.

Bilateral Integration and Crossing Midline

- Can the student move his or her legs from side to side across the midline when transporting a beanbag from the floor to the box?

Position the box at the student's midline. As the student is able, gradually move the box a little further to the side.

Fine Motor

- Can the student scoop ducks out of the water using a slotted spoon?
- When dropping ducks onto the paper, does the student rotate his or her hand and forearm while holding the slotted spoon?

Give a hand-over-hand assist if necessary to help the student get the sensation of turning his or her hand over to turn the spoon. After practicing, the student should be able to tip the spoon so that the duck falls off.

Windy Days

Materials

- 1 sheet of 9" x 12" (23 cm x 30 cm) construction paper in various colors per student
- approximately 1 yard (1 m) patterned cotton fabric
- approximately ½ yard (.5 m) red cotton fabric
- approximately ½ yard (.5 m) blue cotton fabric
- two 12" (30 cm) square scarves per student
- cardboard or poster board for patterns
- 1 cotton ball per student
- 1 windsock per student
- 1 pinwheel per student
- masking tape
- string

Teacher Preparation

1. Tear patterned fabric into approximately 2" x 24" (5 cm x 61 cm) strips to be used for kite tails.
2. Tear red and blue fabric into 1" x 15" (2.54 cm x 38 cm) strips. These strips will be tied around students' wrists to help them identify right and left hands when scarf tossing.
3. Prepare diamond-shaped kite patterns for each student. Use cardboard, old cereal boxes, or poster board.

Directions to Students

Cotton Balls

1. Do you think you are strong enough to blow this cotton ball across the floor? I'm going to put a strip of masking tape on the floor; this is the starting line. A couple of feet away I'm going to put another strip of masking tape; this is the finish line.
2. When it's your turn, lie down on your tummy and put the cotton ball on the starting line. Blow the cotton ball toward the finish line. You can move your body forward so you're closer to the cotton ball, but don't touch it with your body!

Pinwheels

1. Let's see if we can make the pinwheels spin around just by blowing on them. Can you make it spin if you hold the pinwheel out at arm's length or does it need to be closer to your mouth?
2. Can you make the pinwheel spin while you're sitting in a chair, or standing, or lying on your tummy?

Windy Days (cont.)

Directions to Students (cont.)

Windsocks

1. Windsocks let us know which way the wind is blowing. Let's take our windsock outside and hold it up in the air to see if the wind is blowing.

2. We can make air go through the windsock by holding the windsock out away from our body and moving quickly.

3. Can you make your windsock fly when you turn around? When you run?

Scarf Juggling

1. Have you ever watched someone toss up a ball and, just before catching that ball, toss up a second ball? This is called juggling. Scarf juggling is a little easier than ball juggling. Scarves float on the air when you toss them up, and that gives you a little extra time before the scarves are low enough to catch. Today we're going to play some games using scarves.

2. Before we start juggling, tie a red fabric strip on your right wrist and a blue fabric strip on your left wrist.

3. If I want you to toss a scarf up with this hand (raise your right hand up above your head), I'll say "Red Hand." If I want you to toss one scarf up in the air with your other hand, I'll say "Blue Hand."

4. Gently toss one scarf up in the air with your red hand. Can you toss the scarf up above your head? Watch the scarf as it floats gently down to the ground.

5. This time, toss the scarf up in the air with your Red Hand, and as it floats down, try to catch it with your Blue Hand.

6. Who thinks they can toss the scarf up in the air and clap their hands together before catching it? Can you clap two times and still catch it?

7. You are doing so well tossing and catching one scarf, let's try playing with two scarves! Toss a scarf up with your Red Hand, and then toss a scarf up with your Blue Hand. Catch the first scarf you threw with your Blue Hand, and catch the other scarf with your Red Hand.

78

Windy Days *(cont.)*

Directions to Students *(cont.)*

Tying Knots on the Kite's Tail

1. March is often a windy month and a perfect time for flying kites! Have you ever flown a kite or watched someone else fly his or her kite? What shape was the kite? Did it have a tail?

2. The easiest kite to make and fly is a diamond-shaped kite. We're going to make kites to decorate our room.

3. Choose a piece of construction paper and lay the kite pattern on it. Be sure that you can see construction paper all around the pattern. Hold the pattern firmly so it doesn't move, and trace around it with a pencil. Carefully cut on the lines.

4. A kite usually flies better if it has a tail. Many people tie knots in the tail to help balance the kite better. Use the fabric strips to make kite tails.

5. To tie knots, hold one end of the fabric strip in one hand and the other end in the other hand. Hold onto the fabric while you cross your hands. You've just made an X with the fabric strip. Release your hands and be sure to leave the fabric crossed. Find the fabric end that's on top. Grab hold of that end and move it under the bottom fabric and into the center of the circle. Release the fabric. Take hold of one end with one hand and the other end with the other hand. Pull on both ends at the same time. You've just made a knot in your kite string.

6. Tie four or five knots in your kite tail.

7. Tape the tail to one of the points on your paper kite.

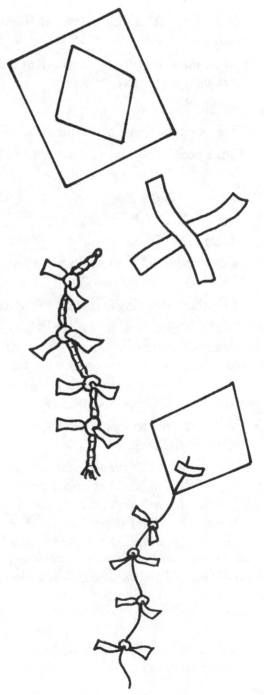

Additional Activities

1. Build and fly homemade kites.

2. Experiment to find out whether kites fly better with or without tails.

3. Watch the trees and try to determine which direction the wind is blowing. Check your prediction with a hand-held windsock.

4. Check the weather each day and graph the windy and non-windy days.

Windy Days (cont.)

Observations for Sensory Motor Activities

Motor Planning

• Can the student toss a scarf up in the air with one hand and catch it with the other hand?

It may be necessary to guide the catching hand upwards when it is time to catch the scarf. Proceed to tossing and catching two scarves only after the student masters tossing and catching one scarf.

Body Awareness

• Does the student maintain a safe distance from other people and objects when running or turning with the windsock?

Delineate a path to follow if the student hasn't developed a good sense of how much space is needed to keep from bumping into others.

Bilateral Integration

• Does student move his or her arm across the midline when tossing and catching the scarf?

• Can student hold the kite pattern in place with his or her helping hand while tracing around it with the pencil in the other hand?

Gently hold the helping hand in place if necessary, but remove your hand before the student is finished tracing to see if the student continues correctly on his or her own.

Fine Motor

• Is the student able to position and maintain scissors with the thumb and fingers in the scissors holes?

• Does the index finger rest on the scissors shaft and help guide while cutting?

Many students have difficulty holding scissors correctly because they have not developed individual finger movements. Provide lots of fingerplays and sign language experiences in your curriculum to develop finger dexterity.

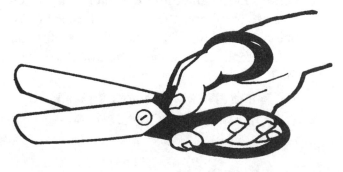

• Is student able to manage scissors, but unable to cut on the lines?

Provide wider lines, as these are a little more forgiving. If student still has difficulty, it's possible that he or she doesn't understand what it means to cut on a line. Place masking tape lines on the floor prior to a cutting activity; these can be zigzag and curved lines, as well as straight lines. Drive cars or trucks on the lines and walk or jump on the lines. When you're sure they understand the concept of staying on the lines, introduce cutting on the lines.

Getting to Know Myself—
Body Awareness

Materials

- 15 short ³/₄" (2 cm) pegs with round tops per student
- Plexiglas™, approximately 24" (61 cm) square
- circle stickers in various colors
- 1 hula hoop or ring per student
- 1 beanbag per student
- 2 body socks per group
- scarecrow pattern (page 84)
- black felt tip pen
- opaque projector
- butcher paper
- clear tape
- play dough

Teacher Preparation

1. Enlarge the scarecrow to approximately 24" (61 cm) tall, using the opaque projector and the scarecrow picture. Copy the outline on butcher paper. Trace over the lines with a black felt-tip pen. The picture needs to be small enough to fit behind the square of Plexiglas. Laminate the scarecrow. Secure the picture behind the Plexiglas with clear tape.

Directions to Students

Shake, Shake, Shake

1. Today we're going to play some games to learn about our bodies. Our first game is called Shake, Shake, Shake. I'm going to name a body part, and you shake that body part to show me where it is.

2. Shake your hand. Shake your foot. Shake your knee.

3. Who can name a body part for the rest of us to shake?

Balance the Beanbag

1. Now we're going to see how well we can balance a beanbag on our different body parts.

2. Who can balance a beanbag on his or her foot? on your head? on your shoulder? on your knee? on your elbow?

3. Now we're going to play a very tricky game! Try to put the beanbag on your head and kneel down without dropping the beanbag. Can you get up from kneeling and walk around the room?

4. Can you sit down in a chair and keep the beanbag on your head? Can you get back up?

5. Where else can we balance our beanbags? How else can we move?

Getting to Know Myself—
Body Awareness (cont.)

Directions to Students (cont.)

Decorating the Scarecrow

1. You have shown me where your arms, legs, knees, feet, head, arms, elbows, and hands are located. Let's find these body parts on the scarecrow.

2. Who can put a red sticker on the scarecrow's arm? a green sticker on the scarecrow's foot, etc.?

3. Who can peel the stickers off the Plexiglas?

Playing with Hoops

1. To play our next game, put your hoop on the floor in front of you. Listen carefully, and I'll tell you which body part to put inside the hoop. Sometimes I may ask you to put two body parts inside the hoop at the same time. Ready? Let's try one hand; two hands; one knee; a knee and a hand; your nose; one ear; one hand; and one foot.

2. What other body parts can we put inside the hoop?

Ghostly Shapes

1. These stretchy bags are called body socks. Please take off your shoes before you step into the body sock to keep the body sock from tearing. Hold the open end with your hands and put one foot inside the sock and then put in the other foot. Pull the material up over your shoulders so that only your head is outside the sock.

2. We will assume different postures and compare. Let's see how different we look from the person inside the body sock.

3. Can you squat down and push your elbows against the body sock? Can you jump and land with your feet apart? Can you put your hands above your head?

Making a Face with Play Dough and Pegs

1. Get some play dough and some pegs to make faces. Roll the play dough in the palm of your hand until you have a round ball. Then, put it on the table and flatten it with your palm.

2. Pick up one peg and put it in the palm of your hand. Without helping with the other hand, can you get the peg out to your fingertips? You really have to coordinate your fingers to move the peg! After you've moved the peg out to your fingertips, put it in your play dough to make a face.

3. Put one peg at a time into your palm and try to move it out to your fingertips. Use the pegs to make eyes, nose, and mouth on your play dough face.

Additional Activities

1. When playing Shake, Shake, Shake, practice memory and sequencing skills by naming two or three body parts and asking students to shake body parts in that order.

2. Help develop balancing skills while students are inside the body sock (e.g., when kneeling on all fours, lift one leg and one arm).

3. Reinforce concepts of halves and fourths when making faces with play dough. Ask students to divide the ball of play dough into halves or fourths and share it with friends at the same table.

Getting to Know Myself—
Body Awareness *(cont.)*

Observations for Sensory Motor Activities

Motor Planning

- Can the student get two body parts within the hula hoop?

It's easier to put like parts (e.g., two hands, two feet) in the hoop and harder to put in two different body parts.

- Can the student kneel and walk around the room with a beanbag on various body parts?

If student had difficulty keeping the beanbag on a body part, try using beanbags that have fewer beans in them. The less full they are, the more they drape over the body part.

Body Awareness

- Does the student quickly identify named body parts and do the action requested?

Some students process visual cues better than verbal cues. Consider providing pictures to go along with verbal directions.

Bilateral Integration and Crossing Midline

- Can the student hold onto the body sock with both hands while stepping into, or out of the sock?

It's easier to sit on the floor while getting into the body sock. Putting the sock on while standing offers those with motor planning intact a great opportunity to coordinate arms and legs while balancing on one foot.

Tactile Awareness

- Does the student object to the gummy feel of stickers or the wet, squishy feel of play dough?

Sitting on moving equipment such as a playground ball, T-stool, or rocker tilt board while working with these textures sometimes distracts student's attention from the unpleasant tactile sensation and allows them to handle these items momentarily.

Fine Motor

- Can the student hold the peg within the palm of his or her hand and move it out to the fingertips without the assist of the other hand?

It's easier for some students to move a cosmetic foam wedge or small 1" (2.54 cm) cube of foam sponge from palm to fingertips than it is to move pegs out to fingertips.

- Can the student roll the play dough into a ball?

Rolling play dough into a ball is a great way to help develop the palms for handling pencils and scissors. Help student by guiding the hands around and around. Release your hands and give the student a chance to continue independently.

Getting to Know Myself—
Body Awareness (cont.)

Scarecrow

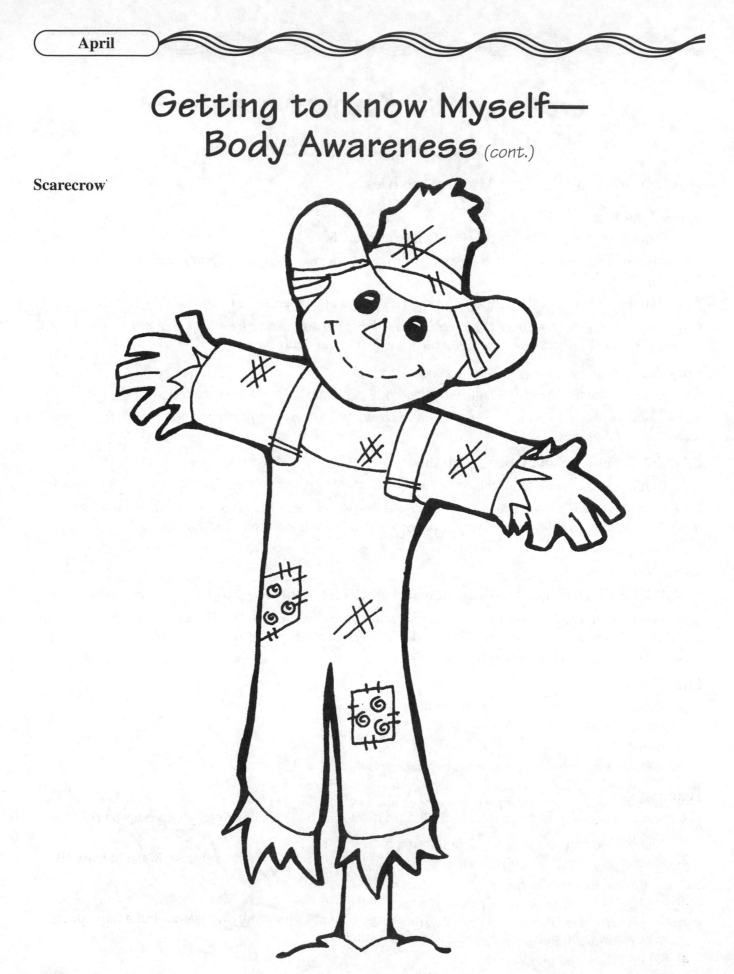

84

Flowers

Materials

- multisensory balls—enough small balls 2½" (7 cm) to fill 2 copy paper boxes (balls are similar to those found in ball rooms)
- 3 yards (3 m) stretchy polyester fabric
- 5 small plastic pitchers or plastic measuring cups with pouring spouts
- plastic storage container, approximately 12" x 18" (30 cm x 46 cm)
- five 8 oz. (240 mL) plastic beverage glasses
- one 8 oz. (240 mL) beverage glass per student
- 5 plastic teacups from children's dish set
- large plastic storage container
- How a Plant Grows work sheets for each student (page 89)
- square of Plexiglas™, approximately 24" (61 cm)
- ⅔ yard (61 cm) cotton fabric for streamers
- ½ cup (120 mL) chocolate pudding per student
- one bag of chocolate-covered candies
- 6" (15 cm) hook and loop Velcro
- 1 graham cracker per student
- 2–3 gummy worms per student
- 1 plastic spoon per student
- scissors for each student
- large plastic pitcher
- 9' (3 m) clothesline
- 5 large blocks
- pinking shears
- spool of thread
- glue or paste
- 4 beach towels
- play dough
- markers
- water
- beans
- paper strips 6 x 18" (15 x 45 cm) per student.

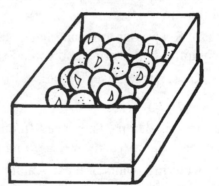

Teacher Preparation

1. Sew a drawstring bag for holding plastic multisensory balls, using stretchy polyester fabric. (See page 71.)
2. Use the pinking shears to cut the cotton fabric into 3" (8 cm) wide streamers. Make at least 10 streamers.
3. Set up a pouring station. Cover tables with beach towels to absorb water spills. Set out plastic tea cups and pitchers and a large plastic storage container for emptying water. Fill a large pitcher with water to be used to fill students' smaller pitchers.
4. Set up beans and play dough.

Flowers (cont.)

Teacher Preparation (cont.)

5. Enlarge pictures of plant growth stages. Cut the pictures apart and laminate them for a whole class demonstration. Place a 1" (2.54 cm) piece of hook Velcro on the back of each picture. Lay pictures side by side across Plexiglas leaving a little space between pictures. Make four boxes on the Plexiglas by drawing around each picture with an erasable marker. Place piece of loop Velcro in each square.

6. Copy the How a Plant Grows work sheet for each student. Cut paper strips.

7. Prepare a pudding cup for each student. Pour approximately $1/2$ cup (120 mL) chocolate pudding into each 8 oz. (240 mL) plastic glass.

Directions to Students

A Seed Grows into a Flower

1. Have you ever helped plant flower seeds? Did all the seeds grow into flowers? Seeds need three things to grow: good soil with lots of nutrients, water, and sunshine. If seeds don't get the things they need when they need them, they probably won't grow into healthy plants.

2. We're going to pretend we're seeds growing into flowers. Each of you will get a chance to climb into my drawstring bag filled with pretend dirt. Other students and I will pat the "dirt" down and around you. We'll pretend to water you, and the sun will shine down on you.

3. Flower seeds grow slowly. First, the stem grows out of the seed. Tuck your chin to your chest as your head comes out of the dirt.

4. Then the stem gets longer. Keep your arms and hands close against your trunk as you slowly stand up. As you stand, slowly unfold your arms and spread your hands. Your hands are the leaves.

5. Lift up your head so we can see the flower's face!

Pouring Water

1. Some plants like the soil to stay damp. They need frequent watering. Other plants like the soil to dry out before being watered again. Today we're going to practice pouring water.

2. We'll pretend that we're watering plants in these small teacups and larger plastic glasses. Try to fill the cup or glass up to the top without letting it spill over!

Flowers Blowing in the Wind

1. When the wind blows gently, what happens to plants? That's right—they sway. If it's a gentle wind, the plants sway gently back and forth, and stay rooted in the ground. If it's a strong wind, the plants bend more. And if it's a fierce wind, plants are wildly tossed about. Some are even uprooted and carried away in the wind.

2. We're going to pretend to be plants growing out of these wooden blocks. Our feet are firmly rooted and they don't move when the wind blows. We have five blocks. May I have five volunteers to be flowers?

3. These plants have very long leaves. Let's give each plant two streamers, one to hold in each hand.

4. The rest of us will be the wind. Let's see if you can sway gently side to side as we blow gently. If we blow stronger, can you bend and sway more vigorously, but still keep your feet on the block.

Flowers (cont.)

Directions to Students (cont.)

Pretending to Plant Seeds

1. Did you know that a bean is a seed? If we plant it in dirt, water it, and put it in the sun, it will probably grow into a plant. We're going to practice planting beans in play dough.

2. Everyone please show me your index finger. Hold your other fingers down with your thumb. Use just your index finger and push 10 beans into the play dough.

3. When you've finished hiding your beans, exchange your play dough with a friend. Try to find all the planted beans. Did you find 10?

Sequencing the Stages of Plant Growth

1. This picture shows a child planting a seed in the dirt. (Velcro this picture to the left side of the Plexiglas.) Planting a seed happens first.

2. What happens to a seed when it gets the water and sunshine it needs? The plant starts to grow. Who can find the picture showing a plant just starting to grow? Velcro that picture next to the picture of the seed being planted.

3. What happens to the plant that continues getting the sunshine and water it needs? That's right, the leaves start to unfold. Who can find that picture and Velcro it beside the sprouting seed? Planting happens first. Sprouting happens second. Unfolding leaves happens third.

4. Fourth, the flower opens. Let's Velcro this last picture in the fourth spot.

5. You're ready to sequence your own pictures of flower growth. Cut out the four pictures. Try to cut on the dotted lines. Arrange the pictures in sequence, and paste them, in order, on a strip of paper.

Yummy Mud Buckets

1. We're going to be cooks today and prepare a garden fit to eat! Before we handle food, we'll take turns washing our hands. When you've washed your hands really well with soap and water, sit down so we can get started.

2. First, get a plastic glass partially filled with chocolate pudding. Use the chocolate covered candies for seeds. Push them down into the pudding "dirt" with your finger.

3. Worms live underground and make tunnels that keep the dirt loose so roots can grow more easily. Poke these gummy worms down deep.

4. Many gardeners put wood chips or mulch on top of the soil to help keep the ground water from evaporating. Crush a graham cracker in your hands and sprinkle the crumbs on top of your garden. Time to eat!

Flowers (cont.)

Additional Activities

1. Read Ruth Krauss' book, *The Carrot Seed,* and plant carrot seeds. Graph the number of days it takes for the seeds to sprout. Plant other vegetable seeds. Do different vegetable seeds take longer to sprout?

2. Talk about the water cycle. Fill various containers, shallow and deep, with the same amount of water. Set containers out in the sun to find out which evaporates faster. Graph the number of days it takes for the water to evaporate from each container.

Observations for Sensory Motor Activities

Motor Planning

- Can student hold onto the drawstring bag, balance on one foot, and independently step into the bag of balls?

If necessary, hold student's hands on top of the bag to encourage him or her to coordinate his or her hands and feet.

Body Awareness

- Does student remain on the block while swaying side to side, "blowing in the wind?"

If not, provide a larger block to stand upon. Decrease the block size as student demonstrates the ability to sway, keeping feet on the block.

Bilateral Integration and Crossing Midline

- Does student move the streamer across his or her trunk or just move it out to one side of his or her body?

If student has difficulty crossing the midline, play lots of games like Simon Says where you ask them to jump up and land on crossed legs, touch opposite shoulders, etc.

Tactile Awareness

- Does the student calm down when multisensory balls are firmly pressed against his or her arms, legs, and back?

Students who enjoy deep pressure might attend better if given deep pressure to shoulders and back when they are agitated or unfocused.

Fine Motor

- When pouring water into small teacups, does the student fill the cup without spilling water over the top?

It's easier to pour from a small pitcher into a larger cup. As student develops more skill, either increase the size of the pitcher or decrease the size of the cup.

April

How a Plant Grows

Direction: Cut out the four pictures, arrange them in order, and glue them onto the strip of paper provided.

Rainy Day Play

Materials

- 1 large terry cloth towel per group of 4–5 students
- 1 plastic bowl or food container per student
- laminated house outlines for each student
- 2 pairs of over-the-shoe rain boots
- 1 plastic eye dropper per student
- 5–6 old blankets or flat sheets
- 5 hula hoops or plastic rings
- 2 child-sized raincoats
- 2 child-sized rain hats
- plastic toys to wash
- 4 cellulose sponges
- tables and chairs
- bucket of water
- 10 washcloths
- hand towels

Teacher Preparation

1. Fill a bucket half full of warm water.

2. Create a house outline for each student. Laminate the houses.

3. Lay out the beach towels on the floor, and place the laminated house pictures on the towels approximately 5" (13 cm) from the edges of the towel. Space houses so that students can stand by a house without bumping their neighbor's elbows.

4. Fill bowls or food containers ¹/₂ full of water.

5. Cut sponges into 1" (2.54 cm) squares.

Directions to Students

Dressing up to Play in the Puddles

1. Sometimes it's fun to put on our rainy-day clothes and go outside to play in the rain and puddles. We're going to make pretend puddles with these hula hoops. Who will help me lay these out in two lines on the floor?

2. We need to divide into two teams. Let's go around the circle and count off—1, 2, 1, 2, etc. All the **1s** line up in front of this line of hula hoops. All the **2s** line up in front of the other line of hoops.

3. We need to get dressed in our rain gear before we play in the "puddles." I'll put a raincoat, rain hat, and a pair of rain boots beside the first person in each line. The first person in line puts on the rain gear, jumps with two feet together into each hoop, and then turns around and jumps back through each hoop.

4. When you finish jumping in puddles, you'll need to take off your rain gear and give it to the next person in your line. Then you can dry off! Use the hand towel to dry your arms and legs. Be sure to dry off all the water.

90

Rainy Day Play *(cont.)*

Directions to Students *(cont.)*

Blanket Houses

1. Sometimes when it rains really hard, we just want to stay indoors and play. On those days, it's fun to gather up old blankets and sheets and drape them over the furniture to form blanket houses.

2. Help me drape these blankets over the tables and chairs. We're going to see how many ways we can travel through our blanket houses.

   Can you crawl forward? backward?

   Can you squat down and hold your ankles with your hands as you duck-walk under the blankets?

   Can you crab-walk through the house?

   Can you slither on your tummies?

   How else can you move through the blanket houses?

Cleaning House

1. When we can't go outside to play, we often have a lot of extra energy that we need to use. Let's use up that extra energy to tidy up our room.

2. Let's start by washing our tables. Dip the wash cloth into the pail of warm water. Keep the wash cloth over the bucket while you wring out the extra water. (Demonstrate squeezing out excess water.)

3. Here are some plastic toys that need to be washed. We're going to use these little sponges to wash them. We're going to hold our sponges in a special way. Tap your thumb pad to the pads of your long and index fingers. Tap, tap, tap! Now put the sponge between these same fingers and try to keep it there while you wash these toys.

It's Raining All Over the Town

1. Sometimes the rain clouds are so large that the rain falls over the whole town at the same time.

2. Today it's going to rain all over our town.

3. We're going to use these eyedroppers to help us make rain. Let's practice using the eyedroppers before we drop rain on our houses. Squeeze the bulb of the eyedropper. Keep squeezing while you dip the eyedropper into the container of water. Keep squeezing. Watch the eyedropper fill with water. As it does, loosen your grip on the bulb, but don't let go. Hold the bulb gently between your fingers without squeezing so that the water stays inside the eyedropper. Squeeze the bulb gently and release so that only one drop of water falls back into the water container. Keep practicing!

4. It's time to rain on our town. Please find a house and stand with your feet touching the edge of the towel.

5. Stand with your arm out in front of you and your hand directly above a house. Squeeze the bulb gently and quickly release so that only one drop of water falls onto the house. It's a very gentle storm—only one drop falls at a time on each house.

Rainy Day Play *(cont.)*

Additional Activities

1. Make rain tubes by pounding one-inch (2.54 cm) long nails in a spiral pattern into empty cardboard potato chip tubes. Add ¼ cup (60 mL) of rice or beans and replace the plastic cap. Secure the cap with masking tape. Turn the tube upside down and listen to the gentle rain sound. Use rain tubes to accompany songs about rain.

2. Rainy days are great days to bake cookies and make homemade soup.

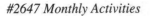

Observations for Sensory Motor Activities

Motor Planning

- Can the student think of ways to secure blankets so they don't fall off the furniture?

Give a suggestion or two and then allow the student time to experiment.

Body Awareness

- Can the student put on a raincoat unassisted?
- Can the student move through the blanket houses without pulling down the "walls"?

Rebuilding the houses is a good way to reinforce the concept of cause and effect. If student repeatedly pulls down the blankets while crawling through the house, try putting weight cuffs on his or her wrists and ankles to draw the student's attention to where his or her arms and legs are in space.

Bilateral Coordination and Crossing Midline

- Does the student move his or her arm in a large, side-to-side arc when washing tables?

Provide many opportunities to move arms side to side, e.g., pretend arms are windshield wipers cleaning the windows while singing "The wipers on the bus go swish, swish, swish" etc.

Fine Motor

- Can the student squeeze wet wash cloths until they are damp dry?

If not, start with smaller pieces of fabric and gradually increase the size of the cloth until student can handle washcloths.

- Can the student squeeze an eyedropper gently enough to allow only one drop of water to fall out at a time?

This takes lots of practice, but is well worth the time spent. If student develops a sense of pressure, he or she will hopefully hold pencils lightly, and his or her hands won't tire as quickly when writing.

92

Picnic

Materials

- plate, cup, fork, knife, spoon, and napkin for each student
- 1 sandwich size resealable bag for each student
- 12" x 18" (30 cm x 46 cm) piece of construction paper per student
- 5" x 7" (13 cm x 18 cm) index cards, one per student
- 1 graham cracker per student
- empty film canisters
- black felt-tip pen
- laminating paper
- scooter boards
- peanut butter
- plastic ants
- tablecloths
- backpacks
- quarter

Teacher Preparation

1. Make place mats for each student using construction paper. Trace a place setting with a felt tip pen; include a plate, a cup, a napkin, a fork, a knife, and a spoon on each mat. Laminate each mat.
2. Fill one plastic film canister for each student ½ full with peanut butter and secure the lids.
3. Place one graham cracker in a resealable bag for each student and seal.
4. Place plastic ants into an empty film canister and secure the lid.
5. Make circle templates on index cards to help count plastic ants. Trace around the quarter to make 10 circles on each index card for each child.
6. Set out the following picnic items in separate stacks on a table: cups, plates, napkins, forks, knives, spoons, resealable bags with graham crackers inside, film canisters with peanut butter, and the film canister with plastic ants.

Directions to Student

Going on a Picnic

1. People enjoy eating outdoors when the weather starts getting warmer. Today we're going to pack a snack in our backpack, get on our scooter board, and "ride" to the picnic ground. We will take turns until everyone has arrived at the picnic blanket.
2. To go on this picnic, get one item from each of the stacks and place them in a backpack. Be sure to place the graham cracker on top of the other items so it doesn't get crushed! When one item from each stack is in your pack, zip it up and put it on your back.
3. Travel to the picnic area on a scooter board. Lie down on the scooter board on your tummy and try to use just your arms to propel yourself forward. Keep your legs up off the ground so your feet don't drag!

Picnic *(cont.)*

Directions to Students *(cont.)*

Going on a Picnic *(cont.)*

4. Try to travel around the tablecloth without rolling over or touching the edges.

5. It's time to set up your area. Get off the scooter board, take off your backpack, and lay out your picnic items. Make sure to match your eating utensils, plate, cup, and napkin to the outlines on the place mat.

6. Take turns with the backpacks and scooter boards. While you wait, set up your place mats for a snack.

7. We're going to have peanut butter graham crackers for our picnic snack. Gently spread the peanut butter on your cracker. Try not to break the cracker. When everyone has finished spreading a cracker, we'll enjoy our snack.

The Ants Invade

1. No picnic is ever complete without a few ants. Thank goodness they waited until we finished our peanut butter crackers! I'll toss them onto the tablecloth.

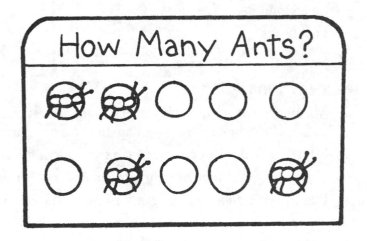

2. Let's find out how many ants there are. Here is a template for each of you. There are 10 circles on each template. Put one ant inside each circle. If you run out of spaces on your template, offer your neighbor your extra ants.

3. I hope we found all the ants! Let's count by 10s to find out how many ants invaded us today!

4. Time to put those ants away. Here's a film canister for each of you. Hold the film canister in one hand. Pick up one ant in the other hand. Without using the other hand, try to move the ant so it hides under your ring and little fingers. Now try to pick up another ant with the same hand. Time to put those two ants into the film canister. The one between your thumb and index finger is easy to put away. Can you get that ant out from under your ring and little finger and out to your fingertips? That's tricky, isn't it? Keep going until you've put all the ants back into the film canisters.

Additional Activities

1. Review proper hand washing techniques. Talk about table manners before going on your picnic. Discuss waiting to eat until everyone is ready, waiting at the table until everyone has finished eating, and cleaning up after ourselves.

2. Set up obstacles on the road to the picnic grounds. Maneuvering around boxes and chairs, under tables, and through a cardboard tunnel are fun and help students develop motor planning.

Picnic (cont.)

Observations for Sensory Motor Activities

Motor Planning

- Can the student maneuver the scooter board around the tablecloth without running over the cloth?

If the student has difficulty with this, place chairs at corners to help establish boundaries. Remove the chairs as student improves.

- Can the student pick up one item from each stack? Can student move from left to right?

If the number of items is confusing, start with fewer items to pack–for example, a napkin, graham cracker in bag, peanut butter in canister, and a utensil.

Body Awareness

- Can the student position his or her tummy in the middle of the scooter board and adjust to balance on the scooter board when necessary?

If difficult, center student's tummy on the scooter board so that he or she will get the sensation of moving from the most balanced position possible.

- Can the student move on the scooter board using only his or her hands?

If the student is using his or her feet to move, try using a fabric sling and lifting his or her legs slightly off the ground.

Bilateral Integration and Crossing Midline

- Can the student stabilize the backpack with one hand while using the other hand to put items in or take items out of the backpack?

If the student does not automatically use his or her second hand to hold the backpack open, take hold of his or her hand and position it on the backpack.

Tactile Experiences

- Does the student object to the feel of peanut butter on his or her fingers?

If the student is overly sensitive to this or other tactile sensations, try some of the activities listed on page 6 and 7.

Fine Motor

- Does the student use just his or her fingertips to pick up the plastic ants?
- Can the student hold an ant under the ring and little fingers while picking up another ant with his or her thumb and index fingers?

If difficult, the ants may be too small for the student to manipulate. Small, 1" (2.54 cm) squares of foam sponge are usually easier to work until the student's hands gain more dexterity.

Spring Has Sprung

Materials

- 2 strips of fabric 6' x 3" (1.8 m x 8 cm)
- 2 butterfly finger puppets
- 2 pillowcases
- 1 hard-boiled egg per student
- egg coloring kit
- vinegar
- wire egg-coloring holders
- 2¼ cups (540 mL) flour
- ½ cup (120 mL) salt
- 1 teaspoon (5 mL) cream of tartar
- 2 packages unsweetened Kool-Aid™
- ½ cup (120 mL) oil
- 2 cups (480 mL) boiling water
- 10 plastic ducks (similar to plastic counting bears)

Teacher Preparation

1. Make play dough. Mix flour, salt, cream of tartar, and unsweetened Kool-Aid together. Add oil and boiling water and blend together. Knead dough thoroughly when cool enough to handle. Store when completely cool.

2. Hide each plastic duck in play dough. Put the duck hidden in play dough into a plastic egg.

3. Hard boil eggs and mix egg-coloring dyes according to the directions on the package.

Directions to Students

The Life Cycle of a Butterfly

1. Butterflies lay eggs that hatch into caterpillars. Caterpillars are caterpillars for only a short period of time. When they have eaten enough and grown large enough, they wrap themselves up in a cocoon that they spin. While inside the cocoon, they change into beautiful butterflies. Let's pretend we're caterpillars and act out their life cycle.

2. Let's start with one student pretending to be a caterpillar. Who will volunteer to be our first caterpillar?

3. Get on the floor on your tummy and crawl along, munching leaves until you've grown very fat.

4. It's time to spin your cocoon. Hold onto one end of the fabric streamer. I'll hold onto the other end. As you turn around and around, the fabric wraps around you and forms your cocoon.

5. While you're inside the cocoon, imagine your body changing into a beautiful butterfly. (Put the butterfly finger puppet on your finger.) It's time to break out of your cocoon. Spin around, and the cocoon falls away.

6. Fly away, little butterfly!

Spring Has Sprung *(cont.)*

Directions to Students *(cont.)*

The Life Cycle of a Frog

1. Did you know that frogs lay eggs in the water and the eggs hatch into—not frogs!—but tadpoles? Tadpoles have tails and swim in the water. They don't have any legs when they hatch. As the tadpoles grow larger, front legs and, then later, back legs develop. As their legs are developing, they lose their tails. Then, they are ready to leave the water. They live mostly on land, but they still like to jump into the water from time to time!

2. We're going to reenact the life cycle of a frog. First, we have to squat down and curl up as small as we can so that we look like a frog egg.

3. When you hatch out of the egg you have no front or back legs. Take turns hatching. Put your legs into a pillowcase and pull it up as high as it will go so that it covers your hands. The pillowcase is your tadpole tail.

4. As you swim, your front legs develop, so let your arms come out of the pillowcase.

5. Swim around a little while longer as your back legs develop. As your tail gets shorter and shorter and finally disappears you can bring your legs completely out of your pillowcase tail.

6. Now you're ready to leave the water. Squat down with your hands between your feet on the floor. Time to jump like a frog. (Hands move forward and then feet jump forward.)

Decorating Eggs

1. People in many countries around the world decorate hard-boiled eggs in the spring of the year. Then they use these eggs as part of their spring celebration.

2. Today, we're going to dip hard-boiled eggs in egg dye. Place your egg on the wire dipper. Carefully place the wire and egg into the dye and leave it there for a minute or two.

3. Carefully scoop the egg out with the wire dipper and let the egg dry.

4. When everyone is finished coloring an egg, you may crack and peel them and have them for a snack.

Duck Eggs

1. Does anyone know how ducklings are born? That's right: they hatch out of eggs.

2. Inside each plastic egg, I've hidden a duckling. Once you've opened the plastic egg, use your pointer finger to remove the play dough from around the duckling.

3. Can you make your duckling waddle around?

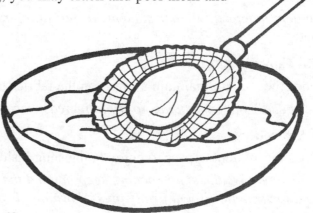

Spring Has Sprung *(cont.)*

Additional Activities

1. Raise silkworms and watch their life cycle.

2. Read *The Fascinating World of Butterflies and Moths* by Angels Julivert. It explains the life cycle of butterflies and moths and has lovely illustrations of each stage.

3. Read *The Fascinating World of Frogs and Toads* by Angels Julivert. The pictures and text help to illustrate the life cycle.

4. Before decorating hard-boiled eggs, show students pictures of eggs decorated by people of different cultures, e.g., Russian, Ukranian. Read *Rechenka's Eggs* by Patricia Polacco, 1999.

5. Visit a farm or local zoo to see newly hatched chicks or ducklings.

6. Read *The Golden Egg Book* by Margaret Wise Brown, a story of a bunny who discovers an egg and is unsure of what to expect from it.

Observations for Sensory Motor Activities

Motor Planning

- Is the student able to keep his or her tummy on the floor while crawling like a caterpillar?

If not, gently but firmly press down on student's back to give the sensation of crawling with tummy against the floor.

- Can the student assume and maintain a squatting position? Can student jump up and get back to a squatting position?

It may be necessary to practice frog jumping in slow motion. First, have the student move his or her hands forward, keeping on the floor, and then jump, feet forwards.

Body Awareness

- When frog jumping, can student maintain space around his or her body, or does he or she bump into other "frogs"?

If the student bumps into other students or furniture, try having a tape line on the floor for the student to follow.

Bilateral Coordination

- Does the student maintain a grasp on the fabric streamer while winding the cocoon?

Gently "knead" student's hands to try to increase awareness of what his or her hands are doing.

Tactile Awareness

- Does the student appear to enjoy being snug inside a cocoon?

If the student enjoys the snug cocoon, keep in mind that when overly distracted, he or she might calm down and focus better if you firmly press down on his or her shoulders or knead his or her arms and shoulders.

Fine Motor

- Is the student able to peel small pieces of shell off the egg?

It may be necessary to peel ½ or ¾ of the egg and let the students finish peeling the remainder of the egg.

Circus Day

Materials

- 2 long jump ropes, approximately 4 yards (3½ m)
- clown outfit—medium to large gym shorts, over-the-shoe rubber rain boots, medium to large mittens or knit gloves, and a funny hat (for each tunnel of hula hoops)
- 6' (1.8 m) PVC pipe, 1" (2.54 cm) in diameter
- giraffe and tiger patterns (pages 102 and 103)
- 2 Plexiglas™ squares 2–2 ½' (60–76 cm)
- 1 yard (1 m) orange butcher paper
- 1 yard (1 m) yellow butcher paper
- hula hoops—at least 5 per tunnel
- black pen used on whiteboards
- black felt tip pen
- opaque projector
- circle stickers
- laminator
- scissors
- hacksaw
- tape

Teacher Preparation

1. Cut the PVC pipe into six 1' (30 cm) pieces with a hacksaw.
2. Using an opaque projector and the patterns of circus animals, trace a tiger on the orange butcher paper and a giraffe on the yellow butcher paper. Enlarge each animal so that it will fit behind your piece of Plexiglas. Cut out the tiger and the giraffe, and laminate them. Secure each animal behind Plexiglas with tape.
3. Blow up balloons for the circus tricks activity.

Directions to Students

Drawing Stripes on the Tiger

1. This tiger has lost his stripes and wants them back! He likes to have his back scratched first. When it's your turn, start on the top and draw the lines from top to bottom.
2. Who thinks they can keep the stripes inside the outline of the tiger?

Putting Spots on the Giraffe

1. You'll see some strange sights at a circus. Here is a giraffe without any spots. Let's help him out.
2. I've brought some circle stickers to class today. When its your turn, please come up and put five stickers inside the outline of the giraffe.
3. How many spots does the giraffe have altogether?

Circus Day *(cont.)*

Directions to Students *(cont.)*

The Clowns are Here!

1. Clowns are always fun to watch. They dress in colorful clothes and make us laugh with their silly antics. We're going to dress up like clowns and do a clown trick. Some of you will hold the hula hoops and some will be the clowns walking through them.

2. We need a group to hold the hula hoops through which the clowns can walk. We'll make it like a tunnel. Hula hoop holders need to stand holding the hoops about a yard (meter) apart. Hold the hoop so that the bottom rim touches the floor.

3. We need another group to be the clowns. The first student in the clown line will put on a pair of baggy shorts over his or her regular clothes, step into a pair of rubber rain boots, put on a pair of colorful mittens, and choose a hat to wear.

4. When you've put on your clothes, walk through the tunnel of hula hoops. On your way back to the line, walk around the hoops. Take off the clown clothes and hand them to the next person in line. Then go to the back of the line.

5. When everyone in line has had a turn to be a clown, we'll trade places and give those holding the hoops a chance to be clowns.

Elephant on Parade

1. Let's all join hands to form a circle. Drop your hands and take one step backwards so that our circle is a little larger. Who will be our first elephant?

2. Let's all sing the "Elephant Song" while our elephant walks around the inside of our circle.

One elephant went out to play
On a warm and sunny day.
He had such enormous fun,
He called for another elephant to come.

3. Little elephant, please call on a friend to join you. Put one hand between your legs to make a "tail." New elephant, please hold onto the tail.

4. When you're called upon to join the elephant parade, stand behind the last elephant in line and hold onto the tail of the elephant in front of you. Use your other hand for your own tail.

Tightrope Walkers

1. Tightrope walkers have to have very good balance to walk on ropes suspended up in the air. They often hold a pole in their hands to help them balance. Before they walk on ropes high up in the air, they practice balancing close to the ground. Let's take turns walking on these two ropes.

2. Pretend that you're walking on a rope that's way up in the air. Keep your feet on the rope and try not to step on the floor! When you've had a turn tightrope walking, go to the back of your line.

Circus Day (cont.)

Balloon Game

1. Have you ever tried to hit a balloon with a bat? There's a trick to holding this bat (PVC pipe). Hold your hands up so that your palms face each other. I'll put a bat between your palms. Keep your fingers pointed up to the ceiling; the bat touches only your palms!

2. Let's start with six students who will form a circle. When the balloon comes to you, hit it with your bat. How many times do you think you can hit the balloon before it touches the ground?

Additional Activities

1. When students have mastered hitting the balloon with the bat while standing, ask them to lie on their tummies facing one another, and to try to hit the balloon while in this position.

2. Following the Drawing the Stripes on the Tiger activity, give each student a tiger outline on which to draw lines. Practice making lines on the tiger prior to a printing lesson. This will help students get accustomed to making lines from top to bottom. It will also help students keep marks between the top and bottom writing lines.

3. After reading Dr. Seuss's book, *It Happened One Day*, ask students to help you imagine a circus. Draw a class mural of this circus.

4. Coordinate the number of the week with sticker art. Ask students to count out the designated number of circle stickers and put them inside their individual outlines of a giraffe.

Observations for Sensory Motor Activities

Motor Planning

- When pretending to be an Elephant on Parade, can the student hold onto the hand of the child in front and offer a hand to the child behind him or her?

Let the student having difficulty be the first or last in line, so he or she only has to be concerned with holding one other child's hand.

Body Awareness

- Can the student duck his or her head and step over the hoops without stumbling?

If the student repeatedly bumps his or her head, try using larger hoops, and decrease the size of hoops as student adjusts to fit through hoops.

Bilateral Coordination

- When batting the balloons, can student keep both hands on the PVC pipe bat?

If difficult, have the student keep both hands on the bat when the balloons are too far to one side. Tie a piece of string on the balloon so that you can position the balloon directly in front of the child whose turn it is to hit.

Fine Motor

- Is the student able to draw lines within the boundaries of the tiger's body?

If their lines repeatedly go outside, make wider outline lines on the tiger. Decrease width of the lines as student improves.

Circus Day (cont.)

Giraffe

102

Circus Day *(cont.)*

Tiger

Summer Days Are Almost Here

Materials

- pairs of matching objects for the feely boxes (ex., 2 seashells, 2 starfish, 2 plastic fish, 2 similarly shaped rocks, 2 sand scoops)
- sand toys—sand scoops, plastic measuring cups, plastic cups/glasses, spoons, etc.
- 5 sheets of bubble wrap, each approximately 2' (61 cm) square
- 4 foam rubber blocks, approximately 1' (30 cm) square
- plastic cereal bowl or cottage cheese carton
- dowel, 1' (30 cm) long with ½" (1.3 cm) diameter
- 20 empty pint (.5 liter) water bottles
- large shallow plastic storage bin
- *Snowy Day* by Ezra Jack Keats
- wide, clear packing tape
- Styrofoam pieces or beans
- 5 pounds (2 kg) sand
- 2 large beach towels
- 15 large paper clips
- fish pattern (page 108)
- colorful cardstock
- 24" (61 cm) twine
- horseshoe magnet
- small parachute
- 15 seashells
- 2 feely boxes
- 5 beach balls
- 10 washcloths
- thumbtack
- scissors

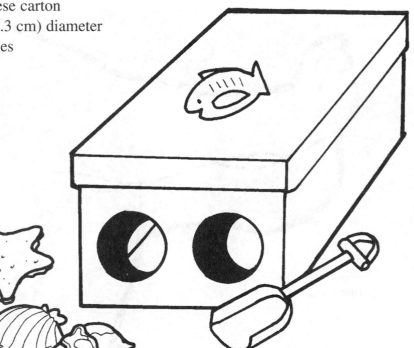

Teacher Preparation

1. Set up a path to the "beach." Arrange bubble wrap strips end-to-end, and tape ends together to form a long bumpy pathway. Lay out the following items in a line on the floor: bubble wrap, squares of foam, large, shallow plastic storage bin full of sand on a beach towel, and finally, the large beach towel and washcloths.

2. Make a magnetic fishing pole and the cardstock fish. Using the fish pattern provided, cut 15 fish out of colorful cardstock and laminate. Attach a paper clip to each fish. Tie one end of the twine securely to a horseshoe-shaped magnet. Secure the other twine end to the dowel with a thumbtack.

3. Make two-handed bats (directions on page 53). Cut off the bottom 2" (5 cm) of the water bottles. On 10 of the bottles, cut four 2" (5 cm) slits from the bottom upward. Push each one of these bottles with slits inside one of the unslit bottles, overlapping the ends approximately 3" (8 cm). Tape securely around cut edge with clear packing tape.

4. Fill the feely boxes with paired items. Add Styrofoam pieces or beans in which to "hide" items.

Summer Days Are Almost Here *(cont.)*

Directions to Students

Walking to the Beach

1. We're going on a pretend trip to the beach today! Let's take off our shoes and socks before we hike down to the beach.

2. The bubble-wrap pathway represents little pebbles, the foam squares represent larger rocks, and here's the sand in this plastic bin. Walk along the path barefoot.

3. When you step out of the sand, step onto the beach towel, and then use a washcloth to rub the sand off your feet.

Playing in the Sand

1. How many of you have played in the sand at the beach? Did you build a sand castle? Did you take sand toys with you so that you could scoop and pour the sand from container to container?

2. I'm going to hide some seashells in the bin of sand for you to find. We'll scoop the sand, using this slotted spoon to find the shells. Gently shake the spoon from side to side so that all the sand drops back into the bin.

3. Keep scooping and gently shaking until only a shell is left on your spoon. Without using your other hand, tip your spoon and drop the shell into the bowl. Keep searching for shells until you've found four shells. Then it will be the next student's turn.

Parachute Play

1. What do you think will happen if the beach ball is placed in the center of the parachute and we all lift our hands up at the same time? lower our hands at the same time?

2. How can we make the ball bounce low? How can we make the ball bounce high?

3. Name a student and make the ball bounce to him or her.

4. Have you ever seen waves at the ocean? The waves can be very high away from the shoreline, but they can be very small at the shoreline. Let's make waves using this parachute. A lot of cooperation is needed. Are you ready to work together?

5. First, take off your shoes but leave your socks on. Then, join hands to form a circle around the parachute. We are going to use our feet to move the parachute up and down. Each student will hold one loop handle with his or her feet.

6. The students on one side of the parachute will lift their feet up in the air while the students on the other side will keep their feet on the ground. Then we'll switch, and those with their feet on the ground will lift their feet up in the air, while those with their feet up will lower their feet to the floor.

Seashore Feely Box

1. There are two shells, two round rocks, two plastic fish, and two sand scoops in the feely box. Using just your hands, reach inside the box and try to find two objects that are the same.

2. Continue feeling around until you have matched all the items.

3. Put the paired items back into the box for the next person.

Summer Days are Almost Here *(cont.)*

Directions to Students *(cont.)*

Beach Ball Play

1. Most times when we play with a beach ball, we use our hands to hit it. This time we are going to use special bats called two-handed bats. One hand holds one end, and the other hand holds the other end.

2. Choose a partner and lie on the floor facing each other, leaving about 5' (1½ m) between you. When the beach ball comes towards you, try to hit it with your bat so that it goes back to your friend. Keep playing.

3. You're doing very well hitting the ball back and forth to each other. Let's see if we can play a cooperative game. Let's all join hands in a circle. Drop hands and take two giant steps backwards.

4. Get down on your tummies and see if you can hit the ball when it comes to you. If the ball is closer to your neighbor, let your neighbor hit it.

5. Do you think we could play this game with two balls going at once within our circle?

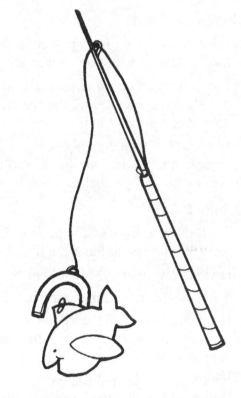

Fishing

1. How many of you have gone fishing? Did you catch a fish right away? Fishermen usually have to be very patient. Some fish are slow to bite the bait on the hook.

2. We're going to go fishing today. Our fishing pole has a magnet instead of a hook. Can you hold your arm out away from your body and catch a fish with the magnet?

Angels in the Sand

1. Children who live in snow country often make angels in the snow. Here's a picture of a child making a snow angel. The picture is in a book called *Snowy Day* by Ezra Jack Keats.

2. What would the sand look like if you were to lie on your back and move your arms and legs away from your trunk and back to your trunk?

3. Let's pretend that we're lying in the sand. Start with your arms against your sides and your legs together. Simultaneously move your arms up over your head while your legs move apart. Now, move your arms and legs back to a starting position. Try to keep your arms and legs touching the floor the whole time you are moving them.

Additional Activities

1. Pour water from container to container at a pouring table.

2. Build sand castles in the sand pile.

Summer Days are Almost Here *(cont.)*

Observations for Sensory Motor Activities

Motor Planning

- Can the student hold onto the parachute straps with his or her feet while raising and lowering the parachute?

If difficult, tie the parachute straps to his or her feet.

- Is the student able to keep both hands on a two-handed bat while hitting a beach ball?

If difficult, tie a piece of yarn or string to the balloon and hold the balloon in front of the student. When student develops better hitting skills, introduce hitting the balloon back and forth between students.

Body Awareness

- When forming a circle, does student maintain his or her own space or bump into others?

If bumping into neighbors interferes with play, try placing rubber footprints on the ground upon which the student can stand.

Bilateral Integration/Crossing Midline

- Can the student hold a container in each hand and pour from one to the other?

It takes lots of play in the sand pile or at the water/sand table to develop accuracy pouring.

Tactile Awareness

- Is the student able to use only the sense of touch to locate like-objects hidden in the feely box?

Provide many opportunities to identify objects using only one hand at a time. Using only one hand at a time encourages students to develop greater dexterity.

Fine Motor

- Is the student able to keep the seashell on the slotted spoon while gently shaking the spoon?

Some students shake the spoon so vigorously that the shells fly off. Place your hand on top of the student's hand and guide the shaking movement. Release your hand as the student develops skill.

Summer Days are Almost Here (cont.)

Fish

108

Water Play

Materials

- sponges
- dishpan
- dish soap
- butcher paper
- 4 squirt bottles
- T-stool or large ball
- 4 child-sized beach buckets
- 1 plastic eyedropper per student
- 1 plastic counting bear per student
- bubbles and wands for each student
- two 8-ounce (240 mL) plastic cups per student
- target and string to attach target to fence or wall
- muffin tins to be shared by groups of 2–3 students
- 2 containers, large enough to hold approximately 8 gallons (30 liters) of water

Teacher Preparation

1. Fill one large container with water and place it outdoors on the grass, with beach buckets beside it. Place another large empty container about 10 feet away from the container with water in it.
2. Draw a circle on butcher paper. Laminate the circle and hang it on the fence, wall, or chair.
3. Cut sponges into 1" (2.54 cm) squares.
4. Fill half the muffin tin sections with water, leaving the other sections empty.
5. Mix 1 cup (240 mL) of dish soap and 1 cup (240 mL) of water in the dishpan.
6. Arrange squirt bottles and T-Stools or large balls.

Directions to Students

Fireman's Bucket Pass

1. Many years ago people didn't have pipes leading to water faucets in their homes. There were no underground pipes to carry water from a storage tank to our homes and schools. When there was a fire, there were no fire hydrants to supply water to the hoses. Fire trucks held large containers filled with water. When the firemen got to the fire, they stood side by side and passed buckets of water down the line of men. The fireman closest to the burning building got the bucket of water and threw the water on the fire. What do you think they did with the empty buckets? That's right, one fireman ran them back to the fire truck to be filled.
2. Today we're going to pretend to be firemen and form our own "bucket brigade." Line up shoulder to shoulder between the two containers. The student closest to the water bucket fills a beach bucket with water and passes it to a neighboring student. The last student in line dumps the water into the empty container.
3. Designate one student to be the bucket runner to run the empty bucket back to be filled again.

Water Play *(cont.)*

Directions to Students *(cont.)*

Squirt the Target

1. We've all tried to keep our balance while standing on one foot. Today we're going to try to balance in a different way. We're going to sit on these funny one-legged stools called T-Stools and try to keep our balance.

2. Now that you can remain sitting on this stool, let's try to squirt the target with this squirt bottle. Can you squirt above the target? below the target?

Eye Dropper Transfer

1. When we played firemen, we used buckets to move water from one place to another. Now we're going to use little eyedroppers to move the water from this muffin pan space (depression filled with water) to an empty muffin pan space.

2. Press the bulb of the eyedropper and keep pressing while you put the eyedropper in the water. Now let go of the bulb. The eyedropper fills with water!

3. Hold onto the bulb, but don't squeeze! Move the eyedropper over to the empty muffin cup. Now squeeze the bulb to let the water out. Keep transferring water until you've moved it into another muffin section.

Give the Bear a Bath

1. This cup is just big enough to be a bear's bathtub. Let's put the bear inside of it.
2. Now we need to get the water from the holding tank (point to the cup filled with water) to our bathtub.
3. You'll need strong hands to do this next job. We're going to use a sponge to get the water into the bathtub! Hold the sponge with your fingertips and dip the sponge into the water.
4. Very carefully move the sponge into your palm. Can you do this without using your other hand?
5. Put your hand over the bathtub and squeeze very hard. Try to get all the water out of the sponge!
6. Keep sponging water into the tub until it's full.
7. Wash your bear with the sponge. Be sure to get his face, ears, and paws clean.
8. Empty the tub using the sponge to transfer water from the tub to the "holding tank."

Making Bubbles

1. Dip your bubble wand into a small plastic bottle filled with bubbles, or into a dishpan filled with the soap mixture.
2. Hold your arm and bubble wand away from your body.
3. Turn around and watch your bubbles float away!

Additional Activities

1. When students are able to pass one bucket of water without delay, encourage them to start passing a second bucket before the first bucket reaches the end of the line.
2. Ask students to wash small plastic classroom manipulatives using the same techniques used in Give the Bear a Bath.

Water Play *(cont.)*

Observations for Sensory Motor Activities

Motor Planning

- Can the student maintain balance while sitting on a T-stool?

Maintaining balance while sitting on a T-stool helps develop trunk muscles needed for good sitting posture. If the student falls off easily, check the height of the stool. It should be approximately as tall as the distance from middle of the student's knee to the floor.

- Can the student fill a bucket and pass it without spilling?

Filling buckets and passing them is probably a new experience for most children. New experiences force us to motor plan. Observe how quickly the students adjust to this challenge and time the bucket passing. If they have difficulty keeping two buckets moving down the line, wait until the first bucket travels to the end of the line and is dumped before sending the second bucket.

Body Awareness

- Can the student pass a water bucket without bumping into another student?

Being able to pass water buckets without bumping up against a neighboring child demonstrates good body awareness. If children routinely bump into one another, space them a little further apart, and as they develop better body awarenss, move them closer together?

Bilateral Integration and Crossing Midline

- Can the student pass a water bucket across the front of his or her body while keeping his or her feet in place?

If the student moves feet rather than crossing arms over the midline, ask the student to "glue" feet to footprints placed on ground.

Tactile Awareness

- Does the student vocalize displeasure or discomfort when his or her clothes get wet or his or her hand comes into contact with the bubbles?

A student who protests these experiences may need repeated exposure of short duration. Gradually lengthen the duration of activity.

Fine Motor

- Can the student transfer water using an eyedropper?

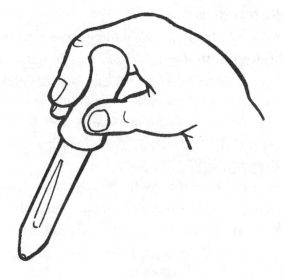

Pressing the bulb of the eyedropper with thumb pad and opposite pads of index and long fingers gives the student another opportunity to practice and become comfortable with using the tripod grasp needed for effectively handling a pencil.

Sources and References

Sources

The following five suppliers carry the items referred to in this book.

Flaghouse
601 Flaghouse Drive
Hasbrouck Heights, NJ 07604
1-800-793-7900
www.flaghouse.com

Folkmanis, Inc.
1219 Park Avenue
Emeryville, CA 94608
510-658-7678
www.folkmanis.com

Sammons Preston
P.O. Box 5071
Bolingbrook, IL 60440-5071
1-800-323-5547
www.sammonspreston.com

Southpaw Enterprises
P.O. Box 1047
Dayton, OH 45401-1047
1-800-228-1698
www.southpawenterprises.com

Sportime Abilitations
One Sportime Way
Atlanta, GA 30340
1-800-850-8602
www.abilitations.com

Body sox—Sportime or Southpaw Enterprises

Butterfly finger puppets—Folkmanis, Inc.

Cones—Sportime

Direct cue hands and feet—Sportime

Gymnastic ball—Sammons Preston or Sportime

Height adjustable balance stool (sometimes called a T-stool)—Flaghouse

Multisensory balls—Sportime

Parachute—Sportime

Plastic rings or hoops—Sportime

Rocker balance board (sometimes called a tiltboard)—Sammons Preston

Scarves—Sportime

Scooter board—Sportime

Therapy putty—Sportime or Sammons Preston

Weighted vest—Sammons Preston or Southpaw Enterprises

References

Ayers, A. Jean. *Sensory Integration and the Child.* Western Psychological Services, 1979.

Baehr, T. *My First Dictionary.* Houghton Mifflin Co., 1980.

Bissell, J. J. Fisher, C. Owens, and P. Polcyn. *Sensory Motor Handbook: A teacher's guide for implementing and modifying activities in the classroom.* Sensory Integration International, 1988.

Fink, B. *Sensory-Motor Integration Activities.* Therapy Skill Builders, 1989.

Haldy, M. and L. Haack. *Making It Easy—Sensorimotor Activities at Home and School.* Therapy Skill Builders, 1995.

Herring, K. and S. Wilkinson. *Action Alphabet.* Therapy Skill Builders, 1995.

Olsen, J. *Handwriting Without Tears.* Jan Z. Olsen, 1997.

Sher, B. *Extraordinary Play with Ordinary Things.* Bob Adams, Inc., 1994.

Young, S. *Movement Is Fun.* Sensory Integration International, 1988.